Hatfield at War

Hatfield at War

The story of life in a small town in 1939–45

by Brian G Lawrence

Published October 2016

Published by Hatfield Local History Society

Printed via www.lulu.com

Copyright © 2016 – Brian G Lawrence

First published by Bel Publications, 1995

Republished with minor revisions by Bel Publications, 1997

This third edition, with additional text and photographs,
published by Hatfield Local History Society, 2016

ISBN 978-0-9928416-6-9

COVER PHOTOGRAPH

Home Guard Sergeant alongside an unexploded bomb in Hatfield
Park – possibly during War Weapons Week, April 1941

ii

FOREWORD

THIS book tells how the Second World War affected ordinary families, what actually happened when evacuees arrived in local homes and how they rallied to 'Dig for Victory', 'Salute the Soldier' or 'Hit the Nail in Hitler's Coffin'. It demonstrates just how much salvage one small town could produce, and makes the connection between Hatfield, Winston Churchill, Stalingrad and HMS *Tweed*. It gives a fascinating insight into how the war changed life at Hatfield House and the significance of developments at the de Havilland Aircraft Co., which made this particular small town a target for German bombers. Here is the Home Front 1939–45 in microcosm, full of the energy, determination, humour and courage of British men and women in wartime.

Author's Acknowledgements

MY thanks to all those who provided facilities for research and made contributions in the form of information, anecdotes and photographs, including:

-   Hertfordshire Archives and Local Studies (HALS)
-   Hatfield Library
-   Mill Green Museum
-   Hatfield House
-   BAE Systems

I am indebted to the numerous past and present residents of Hatfield whose reminiscences have breathed life into this narrative, and I must also thank both Hatfield Local History Society (formerly 'Hatfield This Century') and Hatfield Town Council, whose support helped make this publication possible.

Finally, my thanks to my wife, whose practical help and encouragement were invaluable at all stages in the preparation of this book.

Brian G Lawrence

You never know who's on the wires!

BE CAREFUL
WHAT YOU SAY

CONTENTS

Queen Elizabeth's visit to the Military Hospital, Hatfield House, 1940, accompanied by Miss Richardson (Matron), Lord Salisbury (left) and Lady Salisbury behind him

Patients and staff in the grounds of Hatfield House

ILLUSTRATIONS

PHOTOGRAPHS and other images in this publication are the intellectual property of Hatfield Library, Hatfield House, Mill Green Museum, *The Herts Advertiser* or BAE Systems, unless otherwise shown. Grateful thanks are expressed to these organisations for providing the images and permitting their use.

A S a small boy of two-and-a-half years old at the outbreak of the Second World War, I would describe myself as very much a product of the war years. Children born just a few years earlier, during the first half of the 1930s, must have noticed a tremendous change in their way of life with the outbreak of war. My own earliest recollections, however, are of life in Hatfield during the war. The restrictions imposed on us all from 1939 onwards were 'normal', as I had no earlier experiences with which to compare them.

The author at home, *c.*1938

Although I was an only child, living with my parents in a cottage occupied by my mother's family since it was built some 50 years earlier, I knew it as a house that always seemed to be full. At first it was evacuees— two teenage girls from Hornsey—then a whole series of soldiers attending training courses at the nearby Jack Olding's factory (see Chapter 8). Over a period, we had soldiers from most parts of the UK and at least two pairs from Canada. One of my lasting memories is of one of the Canadians taking the direct route to the lavatory (in an outhouse) by jumping out of his first-floor bedroom window rather than using the stairs. Later in the war, the soldiers were replaced by a series of war-workers; I recall factory workers, bus-drivers and bakers.

At various times during the war, when the bombing was at its peak, we also had relatives and friends from North London who would descend upon us in the evening in order to get an undisturbed night's sleep. On these occasions there were people sleeping in every room in the house, some on mattresses on the floor. There was one memorable occasion when a house full of people was awakened by my mother leaping from her bed on the living room floor screaming that an incendiary bomb had fallen down the chimney. The chaos subsided when someone realised that the empty sugar bag, which had been thrown onto the dying embers of the fire shortly before bedtime, had suddenly flared up to light the room. By the time our Morrison shelter[1] was delivered, fairly late in the war, the demand for floor space had subsided.

To provide some entertainment for our visitors, we always had board-games and cards available, and a dartboard hanging on the living room wall. This proved very popular with the soldiers as it meant that they didn't have to visit The Wrestlers[2] when their funds were low, and I'm sure it helped to give me a flying start in arithmetic.

These recollections and many others come flooding back many years later—my Mickey Mouse gas mask, the disk that hung round my neck bearing my identity number which I still remember (DFEH 30:4) and the ration books, possibly the family's most precious possessions in those austere days.

Despite the very limited range of our diet and the small quantities of certain foods that were allowed (as supplies became increasingly scarce), there always seemed to be an adequate amount of food available in the house irrespective of the number of visitors. I clearly recall ration books, coupons and having to go

---

[1] Morrison shelter: an indoor bomb shelter of cage-like construction
[2] The Wrestlers: a nearby public house in the Great North Road

to the same butcher, grocer or baker each week, but I never felt that we were deprived of any food either in terms of choice or quantity.

We kept numerous chickens and rabbits in the garden and, with no time for sentiment, always had plenty of eggs and additional meat to supplement our rations. We were also fortunate in that my father's work was at a nearby nursery in Smallford growing tomatoes. Therefore, when the boxes of tomatoes were collected for market, it was often possible to change a pound of tomatoes for other items on the lorry. These were usually other vegetables in short supply, but just occasionally an orange or two, or maybe the odd over-ripe and rather black banana. As my father was involved in food production, he became entitled to agricultural rations such as extra tea, sugar and cheese, which boosted our basic rations and even allowed us to pass on a modest amount to our neighbour.

We lived in a semi-detached cottage and another ceremony I recall quite vividly involved alerting our neighbour in the event of an air-raid warning. Whichever family first heard the siren would pick up the poker from the hearth and bang it on the adjoining wall of the living room until there was a similar bang of acknowledgement from the other side—an intriguing ritual for a toddler.

These are some of my lasting recollections as I grew more aware of my surroundings, but without appreciating until much later the everyday changes that people were having to face as austerity took its grip on their lives.

The residents of Hatfield had recently witnessed a good deal of change and development in their small country town between the two Great Wars. Within a couple of years of the end of the First World War, the long-established Brewery[3] had closed, marking the end of an era for the Old Town and its inhabitants. This was followed in 1927 by the construction of the Barnet By-Pass which

---

[3] Brewery: Pryor Reid & Co. Ltd, which closed in Hatfield in March 1920

also had a considerable impact on the Old Town, providing an alternative artery for traffic from London to the North.

The 1930s brought further development in the growth of the New Town with its modern shops and, further along the St Albans Road, the building of the Council Offices and the Court House. More significant for the future of the town was the coming of new industries such as Cook's Corrugated Cases, Jack Olding's factory and, most important, the de Havilland Aircraft Company. Along with this came the new housing estates, Selwyn, Birchwood and the Garden Village, and a significant increase in population.

Situated only some 20 miles from London and on the main road and rail links with the North, it is likely that Hatfield would inevitably have attracted some attention from German raiders when war came. It seems probable however that the recent expansion of the town, particularly the presence of the aircraft factory, gave it greater prominence in the eyes of the enemy. During the autumns of 1940 and 1944 in particular, but also from time to time throughout the war, high-explosive bombs, incendiaries, parachute mines and flying bombs all hit the area.

There were 503 reported air-raid incidents altogether in the district, resulting in the deaths of 34 people and injury to 135 others. Over 1,600 properties were damaged, more than 250 of them seriously. With a comparable amount of enemy activity in neighbouring districts, it will be understood why this part of Hertfordshire remained in a state of apprehension and readiness in spite of being regarded as a refuge by friends, relatives and strangers coming mostly from North London.

Chapter 2   The Evacuees

JUST before the war actually began, children were moved out from London to places like Hatfield, which were regarded perhaps not so much as 'safe' but 'safer'. The southern parts of the county were designated neutral areas from which or to which nobody should be evacuated (e.g. the borough of Watford, the urban districts of Barnet, Bushey, Cheshunt, East Barnet and the Rural District of Barnet) but all other areas were available for the reception of refugees and, by July and August 1939, plans were well advanced although not necessarily published. At the Hatfield Rural District Council meeting on 28 July 1939, the Clerk (reporting to the ARP[4] Committee on the evacuation scheme) stated that an issue of blankets had been notified and they would be stored at the Methodist Chapel. There was clearly a problem about storage in the parishes as consideration would be given to the issuing of a supply to them if suitable accommodation was available and it was so desired by the Parish Billeting Officers.

On 18 August 1939, the *Herts Advertiser*[5] commented on the Chief Education Officer's Annual Report. Part of this was devoted to the provision of education for the children evacuated from London:

> One thing is clear—in the vast majority of cases schools will have to be run in war time on the 'double-shift' principle, each child (native or evacuee) attending one only. Upon this basis and upon the assumption that the numbers of evacuated children expected in each

---

[4] ARP: Air Raid Precautions, est. 1937 to protect civilians against air raids

[5] The full title of this newspaper was *Herts Advertiser & St Albans Times*

area will not be greatly in excess of the present estimate, no difficulty is expected in providing room in the schools. More difficult problems will be those of providing recreation for the children out of school hours and communal meals.

Here, the Education Officer had great hopes of the Women's Voluntary Organisations and does not appear to have been let down.

At that time, there was great uncertainty about the number of evacuees expected in the area as a whole and there was no real way of pinning down exact figures for a particular locality like Hatfield. Each Urban and Rural District, or Borough Council, was responsible for providing figures of potential evacuees, covering all children and of course many of their mothers if the children were very young. In April 1939, the provisional number set by the Ministry of Health to be sent to the Rural District was 3,600. The Board of Education tried to help the school authorities in their planning by estimating the number of evacuees who would be of school age but at different times the fraction altered from one quarter to two-thirds and then steadied at a half.

> Nevertheless, no difficulty should be experienced in accommodating all evacuated children (in school) on the 'double-shift' principle, unless the numbers received are greatly in excess of present estimates.

The weekend before the outbreak of war was a busy one for the people of Hatfield. As reported in the *Herts Advertiser*, thanks to efficient organisation and numerous active helpers, the evacuation scheme was completed with hardly a hitch:

> Notices to volunteer car-drivers sent out previously warned them that they would be needed to transport evacuated children and teachers on the following day. Accordingly, early on Friday, the North front of Hatfield House was reminiscent of a small motor show, while Fore Street was lined with London Transport buses lent by the Board. When the first contingent of children arrived, their first question was, "Where are we?" and only a few murmured, "Never heard of it!" when they were told.

At the Station the Chief Billeting Officer (Mr E C Doust-Smith) was in charge and he was assisted by Mr B H Oliver and Mr C S A Clark. As soon as they arrived the children and teachers were led into the Park and received by the Reception Officer (Mr H J Secker). Then they were provided with buns and hot tea by Mrs M P G Leonard (the wife of the Rector) who was assisted with the catering by many volunteers. The distribution of the parties to their dispersal points in the district was arranged by Mr V J Cull and the transport organised by Mr C S Knowles, both of whom were aided by as many helpers as they needed. Billeting itself, except for one or two minor problems, presented no difficulties.

Perhaps that was true at this stage to the public eye but stories were to emerge later! One Hatfield resident recalls quite vividly the consternation expressed by her parents when one of their evacuees unpacked a pair of gloves. They had been embroidered with the Communist emblem of the Hammer and Sickle. Nevertheless they quickly suppressed their feelings about the little girl's background and she was readily accepted into the household.

The organisation set up to cope with the initial influx was designed to stay in place in case it should be needed again. Meanwhile, Mr Eric Tingey was in charge of evacuation rations and an office to deal with evacuation queries was opened at 13, The Parade, St Albans Road, under Mr W C Wallis—such queries should not be directed to the Rural Council Offices.

A fortnight after this, a notice appeared in the *Herts Advertiser* to say that the children and staff of the Stroud Green School, Hornsey, would like to thank the people of Hatfield and Lemsford for their warm welcome and for the kindness they were experiencing in their new billets.

By 29 September 1939, the reaction had begun. In a leader headed 'Evacuee Problems' the *Herts Advertiser* tried to assess the position:

When the recent scheme evolved by the Government for the transfer of a considerable proportion of London's population to the country as a measure of safety from air-raids was completed, there was unstinted praise for the efficiency and smoothness with which that

9

scheme had been put into operation. Satisfaction then expressed has been endorsed by representatives of the Government who paid an official visit to certain of the local billets this week. Since the evacuees have been installed in their billets some difficulties, not altogether unforeseen, have arisen. Among householders one of the questions that is most commonly asked is, "How are you getting along with your evacuees?" Replies to that enquiry are sometimes satisfactory, sometimes very much the reverse. Likewise among evacuees there is a general comparing of notes as to how they are faring in the homes into which they have gone. Here again opinions expressed vary widely. ... It was unavoidable in the organisation of an exodus on so gigantic a scale that there should have been a certain number of 'misfits' both in regard to evacuees and those upon whom they are billeted. For the general happiness of the home there must be in operation a policy of give-and-take. In the great majority of cases such a policy is operating, and the evacuees in the main are, we believe, tolerably happy in their new surroundings. ... In a considerable number of instances there will be regrets when the period of evacuation comes to an end. ... Many of the children are having the time of their lives. ... As for the cases ... in which there is genuine ground for complaint ... tribunals have been set up and are still being set up for adjudicating. ... One of the most unsatisfactory features of the evacuation scheme is the extent to which evacuees, especially mothers with young children, are returning to their homes!

This was understandable because there had been no serious air-raids and the women felt they would be as safe in London as elsewhere; they missed their husbands and friends and knew they would be happier in familiar surroundings, but there was a suggestion of ingratitude on the part of the evacuees.

There was also beginning to be some dissent about the 'double-shift' system of schooling. The *Herts Advertiser* 'heard' that there was concern among parents where the alternation of half-days or even whole days of schooling seemed rather temporary but might become permanent. 'Many parents' were apparently wondering what would become of their children's education if the arrangements were to last much longer:

Obviously the children are receiving only half the tuition they would be receiving in normal times, and such a state of affairs would be

10

bound to affect them in the future ... children will be unfitted to take their examinations when the time comes for them to do so.

There was a suggestion that local halls should be commandeered for the scholastic use of the evacuees, leaving the local children to put in their full attendances at their own schools.

This suggestion was undoubtedly pursued in order to solve the education problem and, within a relatively short while, emergency classrooms were set up for the evacuee children in several locations throughout the town. These included, at various times, the Tennis Club, the Salvation Army Hall, the Court House, and temporary wooden huts alongside the Council Offices. The resourcefulness of the teaching staff must have been stretched to the limit in obtaining the necessary teaching materials to enable them to continue their work.

The situation in Hatfield seems on the whole to have been less fraught than most, but there were costs to be borne in many different ways. As early as 22 September 1939, an appeal was made to residents for gifts of blankets and footwear that might be useful to the evacuees. (Once again they should be taken to the Methodist Church Stores at Spring Villas, Hatfield.) A report to the Council early in October revealed that some Hatfield residents on whom the children were billeted had immediately purchased footwear for them. There was high praise at the meeting for the way Hatfield householders were taking care of the children but there were a number of cases needing special attention. These were cases where individual householders could not cope with the children billeted on them for medical or other reasons (such as bed-wetting) and it was unreasonable to consider re-billeting them on someone else.

For this reason it was proposed to establish a hostel where they could be centrally housed under constant supervision. The cost of paid staff would be met from the Government's evacuation scheme but the equipping and staffing of the proposed hostel would provide an excellent outlet for voluntary services. By November 1939, a Billeting Officer could report:

> Were it not for the evidence of my own eyes, I should never have believed that in an enlightened England, with a standard of life far in advance of that prevailing in 1914 on the outbreak of the previous war, children were being raised in so unsatisfactory an environment.
>
> The majority of the evacuees in my reception area are from a district in North London where there are no slums in the accepted sense of the term. Yet we have some children from that particular area who have never sat at a table for meals and, before arriving in Hertfordshire, were unacquainted with the use of a knife and fork. After six weeks the children in question are acquitting themselves so well that they would now bring no disgrace upon themselves or their hosts in any society.
>
> Those who at first shied at and refused bacon, potatoes served in various forms other than as chips, and several dishes common in village and middle-class homes, have today developed a natural liking for such foodstuffs and are perhaps forgetting their previous sustenance of fish and chips and 'pieces.'
>
> What is certain is that if these children remain in their present billets for two or three years they will rebel at any idea of a return to 'pigging' conditions in their own homes. Again, we have children for whom toothbrushes have had to be provided and instructions given in their use; some confessed to never having seen a toothbrush before, others to never having had their teeth cleaned. And it is a strange fact that, almost without exception, the teeth of those particular children are excellent and in no need of dental attention.

It should be made clear that the Billeting Officer's report probably refers to a minority of extreme cases and it should not be assumed to be typical of all evacuees. The children evacuated to Hatfield from North London covered a wide range of social backgrounds and their school at Stroud Green boasted a very good academic record.

The evacuees' hostel was established at Alexandra House (on the Great North Road) which had previously been used as a girls' school. By the second half of November, Mr Doust-Smith could state that it was to the credit of the town's voluntary workers that the hostel had been furnished for the low sum of £5—and he paid a special tribute to Miss A Galloway and her helpers. The County Evacuation Officer sent a letter to the Council praising them for their enterprise in starting the hostel. At the same meeting, Mr Bishop reassured the Council that in cases where evacuated children were sent to isolation hospitals, the cost would be charged to the local authority from whose area they came. In the *Herts Advertiser's* report on Christmas 1939, the hostel figured prominently.

> Gifts of Christmas stockings were provided for the children who, in turn, filled Christmas stockings for the Matron and the house-keeper. ... There was a Christmas Tree Party at Alexander [*sic*] House with Mr W C Day in the role of 'Father Christmas'. The Matron thanked all who had helped to make the festivities a success.

In December 1940, a special meeting was held under the chairmanship of Lady Salisbury and attended by representatives of the Council and various local voluntary bodies. They resolved to form themselves into the Hatfield Town Welfare Council to co-ordinate local welfare work. One of the Council's first acts was to agree the setting up of a Rest Centre for evacuee mothers and children at The Cedars, St Albans Road. The Centre was equipped to provide facilities for washing clothes, bathing, sewing, knitting, reading and writing. Later, consideration was given to the setting up of a crèche. The Centre operated successfully for some eighteen months by which time it was reported that the demand had passed, since most women had been absorbed into war-work. Thereafter The Cedars was used as a clothing store.

ARP Wardens outside the Memorial Hall, c.1940:

(L to R standing) Geoff Harradine, Tom Clark, Arthur Nash, George Davidson, Sid Mills, Stan Harradine, Mr Cooper; (seated) William Halsey, Hugh Jenkins (Chief Officer) Len Cull.

Chapter 3   Preparing for the Inevitable

FOR all its willing contribution to the war effort, the local Council was very conscious at all times of the cost to the rate-payers. After all, they represented the house-holders and traders of a comparatively small town and the burden of the war was falling more and more heavily on their pockets as time went by.

As early as April 1939, the newly-formed Hatfield Rate-payers' and Tenants' Association expressed its 'alarm and grave concern' over 'the rising rates and increased expenditure contemplated by the Rural Council, especially as national expenditure was at a level previously unknown in peace time and it was impossible to estimate what they, in the district, would have to pay'. The resolution urged that future expenditure should be limited to vital necessities only, at least until national taxation was at a lower level.

The chief protagonist at the aforementioned meeting was Mr D'Arcy Cayley who began by blaming the Hatfield residents themselves for the existing situation. He recalled that there had been a Rate-payers' Association three years previously but it had died from lack of interest and support. He expressed his determination that the new Association should not meet the same fate.

As far as expenditure was concerned, he saw no necessity for extending the Council Offices when there were buildings available (used by the Parish Council which he contended was redundant and could be abolished altogether!)

Referring to the Council's proposal to purchase a burial ground at a cost of £4,000, Mr Cayley described the cost as excessive. Recreation grounds, he considered, were not necessary, for there was not a house in Hatfield which was not within five minutes' walk of the country. Expenditure on such prime necessities as ARP, a new ambulance and fire-engine could not be criticised, but he doubted the urgency of such things as community centres, a swimming pool and a crematorium.

> The idea of a crematorium is too ludicrous to merit one moment's attention. ... I agree that community centres are very good things to have, but they are not essential. I admit too that there is a demand for a swimming pool, but remember that it requires only one man's wish to create a demand. If we had a swimming pool, I am convinced that not five per cent of the population would ever use it!

It is clear from such statements that even before the outbreak of war with its new and unusual demands upon the budget, the Council had great difficulty making ends meet and pacifying the rate-payers. Similar headaches were experienced at County level where the Herts Public Assistance Committee sought to organise a £30,000 scheme of Air Raid Protection for hospitals, institutions and children's homes throughout the area in June 1939.

With regard to Wellfield[6], which was at that time a rest-home for the elderly, Sir David Rutherford (the Chairman) expressed his regret that the Ministry had not seen fit to approve the full cost of the proposed scheme which was £175. It had included some kind of construction for protection against light incendiary bombs (costing approximately £50). This, the Ministry was disinclined to allow.

The matter did not end there but was followed up at a meeting of the Barnet Guardians' Committee where Mrs Hopkyns protested about the refusal of the Ministry to agree:

---

[6] Wellfield Old People's Home, originally Hatfield Workhouse

> The reason given for the decision was that Wellfield was in close proximity to the de Havilland works and would be comparatively safe in view of the anti-aircraft precautions.

Mrs Hopkyns pointed out that in addition to being near the aircraft works, Wellfield was comparatively near the Brookmans Park wireless station and quite close to an important railway viaduct and junction:

> The people who gave this decision do not realise our position and I don't think they have been to see the place. We are responsible for the lives of these old ladies, and in addition to that we have been scheduled to receive patients from the London Hospital and the Royal Free Hospital in the event of trouble.

It was also suggested that such a place as de Havilland's would be a potential target for bombs! It was reported that the Clerk had written to protest against the Ministry's decision.

In July 1939, the imminence of war caused the County to take a further look at its budget, deferring the seeking of tenders for approved capital expenditure until late September or October 'so that the Council may act in accordance with the conditions prevailing at that time' and setting an increased County Rate to cover rising costs. Once more, Lord Salisbury uttered a strong plea for economy in local expenditure, especially at a time when such heavy demands were being made to meet the cost of defence.

A week or so later, the Council Offices were again under discussion in Hatfield. Their extension and the provision of a basement shelter to be used as an ARP control room had already been sketched. It was proposed to extend the offices along the Stonecross Road frontage and at the same time provide a basement shelter that would adjoin and link up with the existing basement. The area of the basement would be approximately 760 square feet and the estimated cost of the work was being obtained.

An ARP Committee meeting had preceded that of the Council, and authority had been given for the erection of four warden pill-box shelters at the following locations:

- junction of Wellfield Road on the Barnet By-Pass
- land at the rear of the Westminster Bank in Old Hatfield
- Brookmans Park Hotel
- Welham Green or Essendon

By the second half of September 1939, the War was a reality and all planned housing development was postponed. This chiefly affected two housing schemes in Essendon and Hatfield which would not proceed.

Fuel rationing had arrived with the Fuel and Lighting Order which took effect on 1 October. 'Fuel' included coal, coke, gas and electricity, and all consumers except for factories using over 100 tons were subject to government control unless they used less than 2 tons of solid fuel a year or obtained their gas supply through a slot-meter. To deal with the administration of a very complex system, each locality had its Fuel Overseer who, in Hatfield, was Mr W C Essex, with an office temporarily situated at the Council Offices. An Advisory Committee for Fuel was also set up and the members were Mr C Knowles (Chairman) and Messrs W T Gray, H W Gregory, L C Sherriff and A Warrick.

At this time, there began the 'saga of the shelters', which continued throughout the war as circumstances stirred public opinion. On 22 September 1939, The *Herts Advertiser* received a copy of a letter sent by the Secretary of the Hatfield Branch of the National Amalgamated Furnishing Traders Association to the Rural District Council regarding the question of public air-raid shelters. The letter stated:

> At a Meeting of the Hatfield Branch of the Association, I was instructed to convey to the Hatfield Rural Council the deep concern and indignation of our members on the failure of the Council to provide adequate shelters for the public in the event of an air-raid.
>
> We are not, in fact, aware that there are any at all in existence. If this is so, then the Council have a grave responsibility and one that would weigh heavily on them in the event of a raid. We consider it an elementary duty of any Council to take every possible step to secure the safety of the citizens it represents and we trust that a move will be made at once to provide public shelters.

18

Things were happening with regard to shelters, as the Parish Council was assured early in October when it was stated that a public shelter was being provided in the Recreation Ground on St Albans Road and that other shelters were in the course of preparation. At the same meeting, there was considerable discussion about ARP volunteers as opposed to paid personnel, indiscriminate payments which undermined morale and the general strain on financial resources if the system was not run efficiently.

At the subsequent meeting of the Rural District Council, there was an attempt to meet criticism of the National Emergency Committee of that Council. In their defence, it was stated that in all fairness they could not be held responsible for certain matters. They were working under great difficulties 'merely obeying Government instructions, and we shall do our work with less friction if that fact is realised in the district'. (Mr Doust-Smith)

When Mr D'Arcy Cayley expressed concern that some residents were not facing up to their responsibilities in the matter of billeting (which could become compulsory if the Council used its full powers), the Clerk, Mr Edgar Cull, moderately defended those who had done their utmost and advocated caution in suggesting people were not doing what they might do. Mr Cayley stressed that he was speaking of a minority.

In general, there was agreement that the ARP arrangements for Hatfield were being carried out with the minimum of expense and thanks were offered to all personnel, including volunteers, for their splendid assistance. The Emergency Committee expressed its confidence that the ARP scheme being evolved for Hatfield 'would stand the test' and stressed the difficulties inherent in organising a rural district the size of Hatfield, covering four parishes. At this time the number of paid wardens in the Rural District was seventeen (out of a maximum permitted number of thirty-three).

In June 1940, the National Emergency Committee was continuing to press for Anderson shelters[7] for residents living near the airfield. With no more shelters available at that time, the Committee urged residents to dig trenches in their gardens and sought volunteers to dig communal trenches near de Havilland's. The Home Office recommended the alternative of strengthening one room in the house as a shelter and materials were made available for this but a number of communal trenches were dug in the Garden Village, Birchwood and on the Poplars Estate (Selwyn).

Incidentally, for purposes of The National Registration Scheme, which was operative from the end of September 1939, the Rural District was divided into twenty-two smaller areas, each with its own enumerator under the supervision of Mr T M Bootland, the Registration Officer. It was the responsibility of each householder to ensure that every person sleeping under his roof on that particular Friday night was listed (including those on night-work) and, on this basis, identity cards were issued. These would later become the means of rationing food when that scheme came into force.

The uncertainty prevalent in the autumn of 1939 was very evident at the November meeting of the Chamber of Trade, presided over by Mr Eric Tingey who was also a member of the Rural District Council. Criticism of the National Emergency Committee was met by reassurances about 'a watchful eye being kept on expenditure' and 'spending only what is urged by the Government', but a letter from the Clerk to the Council showed just how much in the dark everyone was:

> The Government and other Departments ... are themselves dealing with an entirely novel problem, the conditions of which change almost daily. No one can tell, at the present time, what the outcome will be, and it is quite likely the present war will produce, in certain

---

[7] Anderson Shelter: an outdoor shelter half buried in the ground with earth heaped on top of six corrugated iron sheets and with steel plates at either end

circumstances, financial problems for which the existing order of things does not provide.

Getting down to practical details, suggestions were made at that meeting about shops not closing from 1–2 p.m. to enable shoppers to make their purchases in the lunch-hour and about 'mutual assistance pacts' between groups of traders of the same class with a view to joint-action in cases of extreme emergency. As street lighting was restricted, there was some hope that rebate or comparable benefit might be obtained on the local rate for public lighting. Christmas was approaching and the shopping hours were accordingly fixed to close at 6 p.m. for the first four nights of the final week, and eight o'clock on the Friday and Saturday evenings.

In fact, despite the 'phoney war'[8] and all the uncertainties of life, Christmas 1939 seems to have gone well in Hatfield. A very successful concert was presided over by Lord and Lady Salisbury in aid of the Red Cross and St John's Ambulance Brigade, and the Hatfield Goodwill Society made arrangements for gifts of 2 cwt of coal for each of forty old people, 15 pairs of boots or shoes for children, and several grocery vouchers for needy families. There was a 30% increase in the collection and delivery of mail over 1938. The railway station, like the Post Office at Hatfield, had never been so busy.

As an indication that all sections of the community were engaged in 'doing their bit', the *Parish Magazine* published the Rector's letter in February 1940 from somewhere in France where the Rev. Pat Leonard was at that time helping with the setting up of Toc H[9] Centres for the British Expeditionary Force (BEF).

---

[8] Phoney War: the period from September 1939 to April 1940 when, after Germany's invasion of Poland, nothing seemed to be happening

[9] Toc H: an international Christian movement first established in 1915

Chapter 4   Digging for Victory

FROM the outbreak of war, there was an increasing awareness at national and local level that Britain needed to be more self-reliant in the matter of food supplies. With slogans like 'Dig On for Victory' and 'Grow More Food', the emphasis was on bringing as much land as possible into cultivation—and Hatfield was no exception to this. In November 1939, an Allotment and Gardens Association was formed with a nominal subscription, the secretary being Mr A E Hobbs of Green Lanes, Hatfield Garden Village. By 15 December, there had been forty-three applications for ground. An Allotments Committee of the Council was then set up with power to let allotments and fix rentals.

At a County Conference in February 1940, it was stated that, on the outbreak of war, the country was growing only enough food for 100 days out of every 365. It was by then policy to restrict fruit production to existing acreages, boost the production of vegetables like carrots and onions—which were heavily imported (the Government had arranged for a big expansion in potato production)—and curtail the acreage of flowers by 50% on open land and 20% if under glass. As far as gardens and allotments were concerned, the injunction was to 'grow the things you are going to use; if you can't use them, don't grow them!'

At a meeting of the Parish Council at the end of March 1940, it was reported that there had been 80 applications for land, with the number increasing all the time. Work was already proceeding on 55 allotments and the Council was grateful for the help given by Messrs Jack Olding and the District Surveyor and staff in preparing the Birchwood Estate site. Two further sites had been rented, one in Wellfield Road from Messrs Marriott at a rate of £2 per year, and the other near the Comet Hotel from the St Albans Co-operative Society for one shilling per year. To encourage the tenants, no rent would be charged in respect of the first six months and, after that, at a rate of sixpence per rod per year. Allotment holders were assured of lengthy notice after the war ended as it was unlikely that the land would be required for other purposes for some considerable time.

A year later, the Council could report the allocation of almost 150 plots, the acquisition of a further six acres in Wellfield Road and the extension of the scheme to Wild Hill where Mr Wren had been instrumental in securing a site on which nine plots had already been taken. Within two weeks, 30 plots had gone on the new Wellfield Road site and a further site had been acquired opposite the Regent Cinema. This had been pegged out for the use of the residents of Dellfield and Gracemead. By May 1941, the Allotments and Garden Association was planning a Flower and Produce Show for later in the year on the 'Dig for Victory' theme.

The call to increase food production received a very enthusiastic response from the farmers and general public alike. Nevertheless, conflicts over land usage did occur from time to time as illustrated in a letter in October 1939 from Mr Crawford of Birchwood Farm to his solicitor, in which he complained that the War Department had commandeered, without approval, land in the middle of a potato field adjacent to Green Lanes and the Barnet By-Pass as a site for three machine guns. They had also taken land in an adjoining field on which they had erected a tent and constructed a latrine. Initially he was prepared to tolerate this action as the three machine guns had been set up in a straight line running parallel with the rows of potatoes but he subsequently found that additional land was being taken over as a dug-out and the area now extended over more than half an acre.

He went on to set out details of the yield from this land in the past two years and the cost of the manure that had been used in preparation for the potato crop in justification of his claim.

24

He recognised the need to defend the nearby airfield from low flying enemy aircraft but pointed out that there was an alternative site of waste ground within 200 yards of the present site. The solicitor confirmed that a claim for compensation would be justified but, unfortunately, there is no record of how the matter was resolved. It is worth noting that the waste land to which Mr Crawford referred was also taken over as an allotment site soon afterwards and that it continued to be used for this purpose for many decades thereafter.

From the spring of 1940, there was mention of 'Pig Clubs' in Hertfordshire but the idea took some months to grow into an organised scheme. In July, the local press publicised the fact that by joining a pig club, members could be assured of a proportionate share of purchased foods, and they would also have the privilege of killing and curing a pig for their own family's consumption. Pig clubs could insure against the death of pigs through disease or accident, reduce costs by collective purchase of feeding stuffs etc., and arrange for the collection of food scraps. Every parish was to be encouraged in this endeavour and all restrictive covenants and local by-laws concerning the keeping of pigs were in abeyance, subject to no nuisance being created.

Hatfield responded positively to the challenge and in September an appeal went out from the Council entitled 'Your Waste for the Pig'. As in other places, bins were being placed in the streets for such waste as bread crusts, stale bread, other foods made from flour, waste from vegetables and salads, potato and apple peelings, scraps of meat and other table leavings. Not required were tea leaves, coffee grounds, skins of grapefruit, oranges, bananas or lemons, salt, soap, soda or any liquid—the waste should be as dry as possible. In the first four days, more than 16 cwt of food waste was collected.

Collecting waste food in this way became a habit and periodically there were attempts to drum up more, just as in the case of production from the allotments. Although a headline in February 1941 assured everyone that the 'Herts Pig Industry was flourishing' there was still a need for more pig-keepers and extra bins were being put out in the roads in early March so that people could make a special effort over waste. Early in April, a report about the Hatfield Small Pig-Keepers' Club commented on its steady development with eight members to date and sixteen pigs. Some difficulties had been experienced due to a recent cut in supplies of meal, so the collection of household waste continued to be vital. At the end of April, when the whole town made a phenomenal effort in War Weapons Week, there was a successful 'Guess the Weight of the Pig' competition run by the Club.

By the end of 1941, on its first birthday, it was reported that thirty pigs had been sent to market or to the bacon factory, and the number being kept at that point by seventeen members was thirty-one. Clearly they were making a valuable contribution to the nation's meat supply!

Chapter 5   Hatfield House

L IKE most other families, the Cecils were anxious to 'do their bit' for the war effort. Both Lord and Lady Salisbury were involved in many different ways. She is remembered particularly for her indefatigable support and encouragement of local activities, especially those concerned with children, charities and voluntary services. Lord Salisbury was more involved with county and national affairs, but he was not slow to make changes on the Estate which for the first time was given over to a significant amount of arable farming.

The Park lost its golf course which was ploughed up and used to produce crops with (later in the war) assistance from German prisoners. The War Agricultural Committee helped progress by putting drains in the fields. For the duration of the war, the shooting rights were let to a syndicate. The more wooded areas provided a valuable training ground for the local Home Guard and, for example, in May 1943 there was a Home Guard Demonstration in the Park. The 13th Battalion (de Havilland's) marched from Newtown and the 14th (A and B companies) marched from Stanborough to meet in the Park. Lord Salisbury took the salute standing on a farm wagon, flanked by Colonel Allen of the 13th Battalion and Colonel Greenwood of the 14th. The march-past was led by Major Butcher and Major Randall, after which a demonstration of bayonet fighting took place, followed by a mock battle. At other times, open land seems to have been used by the Tank Regiment for practice.

With the real threat of an enemy invasion, precautions were necessary to guard against the possibility of German aircraft or

Home Guard on rifle practice in Hatfield Park

Members of 14th Battalion Home Guard with their adapted vehicle

gliders landing on the stretch of open ground at the South Front of the House. To act as a deterrent, a collection of wagons and coaches belonging to the Estate was assembled and parked on the site, their value being of only minor importance in the circumstances.

The four large cars were requisitioned by the Government and many people believed the same was true of the House, but that was not the case. Several months before the outbreak of war, negotiations were already under way for the House to be used as a hospital. Lady Salisbury had already in 1938 been instrumental in the re-forming of the Herts 6 Detachment of the Red Cross (which had been active in the First World War) and an account of this may be found in *Growing Up in Hatfield before 1945 (Book 4)* by Elizabeth Hook née Bennett. As the Commandant of Herts 6, Miss Bennett (as she then was) recalled that Lady Salisbury 'when war was imminent went to London and offered Hatfield House to the authorities.' But it is apparent from letters in the archives of Hatfield House that protracted correspondence had been going on with the War Office from early in 1939. In any event, it seems that Lady Salisbury's idea of a convalescent hospital manned by the Red Cross was transferred to Bush Hall (on the Hertford Road) as plans for the House developed into what Miss Bennett called 'a full-blown military establishment.' She gives a detailed account of the organisation of Bush Hall and its change from a convalescent home to a hospital dealing with patients evacuated from London hospitals, often at very short notice and treating more than 2,000 patients in all during the war years.

Up at 'the House', as the military began to take over the administration, all the treasures had to be listed and stored against possible damage and it was necessary to do the same in the matter of the furniture. Unfortunately just at the crucial time, the furniture schedule was held up by the sudden death of Mr Johnson, the carpenter, who was the only man who really knew what was what. Largely because of this, letters about the furniture schedule were still passing to and fro between the Estate Office and the military

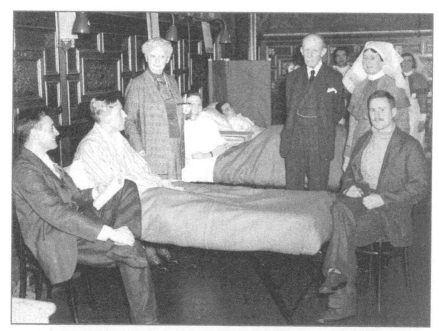

Lord and Lady Salisbury visiting Hatfield House hospital patients

Patients recuperating in stately surroundings

authorities in the early months of 1941. By November 1939, there were 24 patients in residence at the House but they were not at that time casualties, rather they were men taken ill on active service. The family had moved into the East Wing, but even part of that wing was used as an operating theatre. In time, the House was coping with 300 patients at a time (compared with an average of 40–50 at Bush Hall).

The actual agreement between Lord Salisbury and the War Office was not signed and sealed until January 1940 (while the furniture schedule still rumbled on.)

At about that time, new water mains were laid across the Home Farm. There had been some unwanted publicity in the *Sunday Express* on 19 November 1939, stating that the water supplies to Hatfield House which was being converted into a military hospital were 'inadequate' and 'polluted'. The former adjective (according to a very defensive *Herts Advertiser* on 24 November) was applied to one of the independent supplies of water to the premises and 'polluted' apparently applied to the secondary supply—a spring in the centre of the Park. The *Sunday Express* described this as 'unsuitable for the washing of invalids' (apparently it had always been regarded as unfit to drink) and said that 'the alternative supply, provided by the local authority (Barnet Water Company) through privately-owned pipes, is at present considered insufficiently reliable and inadequate for urgent medical needs.' In spite of the local paper's defensive stance and the statement of Mr Secker (Lord Salisbury's Agent) refuting the various points in the criticism, there must have been some basis in fact. Plans were certainly drawn up early in December 1939, if not before, to lay a new three-inch water main (previously two-inch) from the large main at New Bridge on the Great North Road. There were 2,400 feet of piping involved in this improvement, which took place at the beginning of 1940 at presumably considerable expense to the War Office. (The *Sunday Express* had mentioned a figure of £1,000 but this had not been confirmed at the time, the authorities merely assuring readers that 'the House would be made efficient for the purpose for which it had been taken over' and that 'the authorities could be safely entrusted with that matter.')

Publicity was not always adverse. At the end of December 1939, pictures appeared in the *Birmingham Post* showing the transformation of the House into a military hospital. In July 1940, Her Majesty the Queen made the first of several visits to the hospital, and on at least one later occasion she was accompanied by the King.

It was not all plain sailing of course. There were details to be wrangled over, particularly those affecting insurance, as the 24th General Hospital became an active unit. Anomalies occurred, like that of the King James' Room which, upon being de-requisitioned in July 1946, was discovered to have been outside the original requisition and therefore ineligible for de-requisition. Apparently it was not on the original list of rooms used by the military and must have been offered spontaneously (perhaps by Lady Salisbury) so there was no official record of its use and

Notice in the wards at Hatfield House

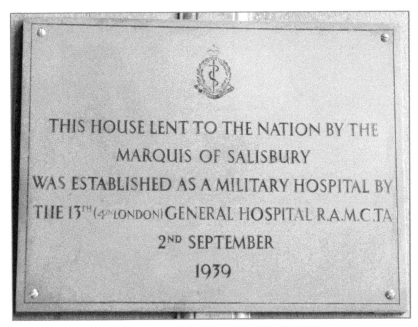

Plaque erected in the Chapel at Hatfield House

no chance of claiming for any depredations. The War Office had no knowledge of its existence!

Difficulty also arose over the speed and weight of military vehicles crossing the viaduct; these had to be restricted because of the damage they were causing. Another area of frequent discussion covered the out-buildings, such as the Riding School, Tennis Court and Old Palace. Designated at different times for different uses, the Riding School ended up as a 'theatre' and was the venue in December 1941 for a crowded concert for sick and wounded soldiers, put on by a Troop Concert Party organised through the County. As often happened, Lord Salisbury was present.

The Old Palace was apparently used later in the war as a convalescent home for Italian Prisoners of War. Some prisoners,

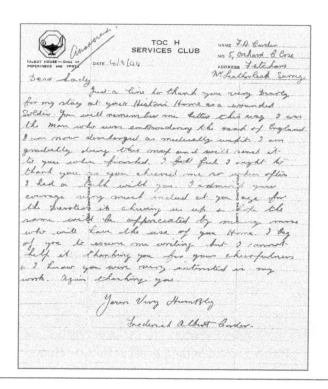

Toc H
SERVICES CLUB

4/9/44

Name F. A. Corder
No 5, Orchard Close
Address Fetcham
Nr Leatherhead Surrey

Dear Lady,

Just a line to thank you very dearly for my stay at your Historic Home as a wounded soldier. You will remember me better this way I was the man who was embroidering the map of England. I am now discharged as medically unfit. I am gradually doing this map and will send it to you when finished. I feel I ought to thank you as you cheered me so when often I had a talk with you. I admired your courage very much indeed at your age for the devotion in cheering us up and hope the same will be appreciated by many more who will have the use of your Home. I beg of you to excuse me writing but I cannot help it thanking you for your cheerfulness & I know you were very interested in my work. Again thanking you.

Yours Very Humbly

Frederick Albert Corder

German or Italian, may well have been treated in the House at times as there seems to have been an incident when a prisoner/patient committed suicide by jumping out of a West Wing window.

In the normal course of hospital routine, unfortunately deaths will occur. The Hatfield Park War Cemetery situated on the Great North Road, just south of Hatfield, exists as a permanent memorial to the twenty-two British and Allied servicemen, ranging in age from 18 to 51 years, who died at Hatfield House between the outbreak of war and the autumn of 1946 when the House was returned to normal use. Among those commemorated is Flight Test Observer J H F Scrope who, along with John de Havilland, was killed when their Mosquito aircraft[10] crashed a few miles away in August 1943.

Before closing this chapter, it is worth recording that despite all the disruption taking place in the Park and in the House itself, cricket continued to be played on the North Front throughout the war years, much as it had over previous centuries. The sight of this traditional feature of English life must have given reassurance to many of the hospital patients as they strolled in the grounds whilst convalescing on summer weekends.

The Hatfield Estate Cricket team, though deprived of many of its leading players, maintained a fairly full fixture list with frequent matches against the Royal Army Medical Corps (RAMC) personnel stationed at the Military Hospital in Hatfield House. They also continued to have matches against teams from neighbouring towns, works teams from factories such as de Havilland and ICI, as well as other military and RAF sides. Frequently, the Hatfield teams were made up of a mixture of veterans and lads who were still too young to be called up, but it is apparent that they were also pleased to welcome guest players from the Military Hospital. Detailed information of these matches

---

[10] de Havilland DH 98 Mosquito, twin-engine fighter and bomber

can be found in *Cricketers and Cricket in Hatfield in the 20th Century (1897–1945)* by H John Gray.

The transformation that took place at Hatfield House was not unusual; stately homes and country houses throughout the country were undergoing similar adaptations as their owners sought to play their part in ensuring the nation's survival. Just a few miles away, at Brocket Hall, arrangements were in hand to equip the property as a Maternity Hospital in 1939 after the London Maternity Hospital in City Road, London, was seriously damaged by bombing. Over the next 10 years, more than 8,000 babies were born at Brocket Hall to mothers evacuated from the London area, but that is the subject of a whole new story in its own right.

LOOK OUT
IN THE
BLACK-OUT

- Before you leave your house, railway station or office, let your eyes get used to the dark

- Before you cross a road, look both ways

- To stop a bus, hold up something white. Do not flash a torch

- Before you get off a bus, tram or train, wait until it has stopped and step carefully

Chapter 6   **Goodwill and Collections**

HAVING done everything in their power to make the evacuees welcome in Hatfield, the local people were not slow to do the same for the patients at Hatfield House. Arrangements for charitable concerts and fund-raising events often included the patients and, from December 1939, they were allocated ten free seats each week for performances at the Regent Cinema. The cinema was a focal point of local leisure activities. On 21 March 1940, the local paper reported on a Police Concert there in aid of Herts Police Charities and, early in April, it was the scene of an entertainment for patients from 'the local military hospital' by the Hatfield Goodwill Society's 'Wounded Soldiers Scheme', which was followed by tea at the Toc H Cottage, hosted by the Committee of the Red Cross Supply Depot.

As the war continued, there was pressure from the workers in the area and this was often expressed in meetings of the Labour or Communist parties such as that held at the cinema in the spring of 1942. On that occasion, a letter was read from the local MP, Sir Francis Fremantle, expressing his support for the war effort and a policy of co-operation with the USSR. It was through pressure from the local working people that eventually, by the end of 1943, the cinema was allowed to open on Sundays for the benefit of the troops and war-workers.

In August 1943, an audience of about 700 turned out to hear a concert by Richard Tauber at the cinema, raising £200 for the Red Cross and St John's Prisoner of War Fund. Another celebrity who took part in one of the charity concerts held at the cinema at this time was the well-known broadcaster Cyril Fletcher, famous for his 'odd odes'. Along with his wife, the soprano Betty Astell, he starred in a concert in aid of the Stalingrad Hospital Fund. There seemed to be no lack of local talent to support the celebrities at such concerts, including Andy Walter (yodeller), Butch Lomax (comedian), Roy Pozzie (magician), Bert Freeman, who had appeared in West End musicals, and Mrs McSweeny, wife of the local pharmacist. She was billed as Madame Eluned McSweeny, a contralto whose repertoire included numbers such as 'Trees', 'I'll Walk Beside You' and 'The Lost Chord.'

From the accounts of local events of the war years, it is quite revealing just how many things were going on, often at the same time. 'Comforts for the Troops' were perennial whether they were being sought by the Red Cross, the Hatfield Women's Conservative Association or the British Legion. Sometimes they were being manufactured by the older girls of St Audrey's School who, in January 1941, despatched 50 pairs of socks to old boys of the school serving in the Forces, and promised another 50 to follow in the Spring. By the autumn of 1942, such efforts had become such a part of life that the annual report of the Hatfield Red Cross and Women's Voluntary Service (WVS) Working Party could claim that 2,131 garments had been made for servicemen in the previous year and 5,491 in the past three years (i.e. the duration of the war so far.)

The young people of the town were encouraged to play their part collectively through the formation of the Hatfield Youth Service Squad. Their good works ranged from visiting wounded servicemen at Hatfield House and providing them with magazines to carrying out domestic chores at Alexandra House on the Great North Road and Honister House in Ellenbrook Lane, both of which were used to house evacuees. One former member of the Squad recalls standing a hot iron on a piece of material and burning a hole in what proved to be the Matron's apron. That was the final occasion on which she assisted at Alexandra House!

Evacuees continued to receive kindness from the town which, in the spring of 1940, was allocated a further 600 out of the 4,000 scheduled to arrive in Hertfordshire. As the year went on and the numbers increased further, the word 'refugees' began to figure more prominently in the local papers. Collections of clothes for those 'bombed out' occurred as in November 1940, when one was organised by the local Women's Section of the British Legion and collected nearly 400 garments in two days. 'Poppy Day' was a regular money-raiser achieving new heights each year. In 1940, the response was described as 'wonderful', £227 being an increase of £60 on 1939. In 1941, it rose for the first time to more than £300.

Flag days and collections in general were well supported, whether for the armed services, benevolent funds, hospitals, Christmas gifts or a wide range of other charities. In August 1941, the Lord Mayor's Appeal Flag Day raised over £220 towards the National Air-Raid Disaster Fund. The collection was made principally by the WVS and uniformed nurses. In May 1942, after £40 had been collected by the WVS for the Marines' Aid Society, it was hoped that 'Hatfield will not tire of flag-days as there are going to be quite a number, perhaps as many as one a week.' It seems the fears were groundless as the joint war organisation of the Red Cross and St John's reported the sum of £1,688 collected during the year ending 31 March 1943.

With the advent of salvage appeals early in 1940, Hatfield began to achieve fame as 'a town which set a splendid example' among Local Authorities which were not taking the matter of salvage as seriously as they might have done.

Under the heading 'Salvage Wardens', the local paper reported in March 1940:

> The Hatfield Rural Council have tackled with practical enthusiasm and strength of purpose the problem of collecting waste paper in the town. Salvage wardens have been appointed ... and the town divided into sectors. The Council have evolved what might be called a model scheme, which when operating fully will enable every householder to contribute with the least inconvenience his share to this movement for salvaging waste paper.

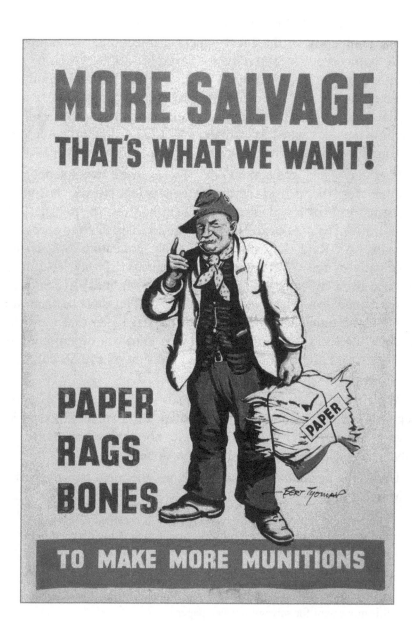

From that time onwards the salvage race was on. By the end of the month, a car had been converted into a lorry for the collection of waste paper. This conversion, like that of a car converted into an ambulance for ARP purposes, had been carried out by the Fire Brigade and Auxiliary Fire Service (AFS) under their chief officer, J J Burgess.

The Clerk to the Council, Edgar Cull, appeared in print, along with pictures of the local Cubs at work collecting and sorting waste paper, to describe the operation and encourage further participation. He was to become the driving force behind the town's salvage campaign with his battle cry, 'there is no such thing as waste paper'. He wrote:

> On Saturday morning we loaded up six tons of waste paper which has been collected, baled and tied up by voluntary helpers with the minimum of assistance from the ordinary staff. Although the salvage scheme in this district is getting under way, there is still very much to be done and the great thing seems to be to get the residents into a salvage-minded spirit where they are keen to see nothing wasted at all. Paper is one thing, but it merely touches the fringe of what can and ought to be done and saved by every resident day by day. It is not the house-holder who has a Spring-clean and turns out a whole heap of rubbish, but the steadily persistent resident who is intent upon saving the daily newspaper and all odds and ends as they accumulate. Residents in this district can obtain all the information needed on application to the Hatfield Rural District Council Offices personally or by telephone to the Salvage Department.

By the middle of June 1940, scrap-iron was top of the salvage list and the scheme in Hatfield was being tested by this new demand. While waste-paper was still coming in regularly, providing on average four tons a week, scrap-iron was more difficult to collect and a system of notification was introduced. To begin with, letters were put through every door in one street 48-hours in advance of the collection from the 140 tenants.

> On Monday evening the volunteers sallied forth with a lorry and a small hand-cart for odds and ends. The result was amazing! All the occupiers in the road produced something in the way of scrap, including stoves, fenders, fire-irons, flat-irons, bicycles, tools, pick-

axes, spades, forks, motor-car parts, nuts, bolts, chains, water-spouts, guttering and door-knobs. Altogether it is estimated that 5 tons of metal was collected. Not all was of first-class value, but a very substantial proportion was just the material for which the Ministry of Supply is appealing. Mr Cull offers the suggestion to other patriotic Councils.

There can be little doubt that Hatfield was in the vanguard of the salvage movement. At the beginning of July 1940, the *Herts Advertiser* commented:

Schemes for the salvage of waste material are to the fore at the present time and one body that is well ahead in this matter is Hatfield Rural Council. The enthusiasm of the Council in launching an intensive salvage scheme has only been equalled by that of the residents who have given it admirable support. The Council have established a depot and local people have made an especially large contribution by way of scrap iron, of which over fifty tons has been gathered at the depot. Thousands of bottles, scores of bales of paper, and innumerable empty tins are stacked in orderly piles ready to be sorted out. A praiseworthy feature is that the scheme is being run by voluntary labour.

Salvage Returns for July 1940 show that the Hatfield District eclipsed all its previous achievements, the total of materials collected being:

- Paper, 21 tons 8 cwt 13 lbs
- Scrap Iron, 50 tons 9 cwt
- Copper, 79 lbs
- Brass, 3 cwt 9 lbs
- Lead, 3 cwt 55 lbs
- Textiles, 14 cwt 74 lbs
- Bottles, 197 dozen
- Jars, 127 dozen
- Bones, 5 cwt 104 lbs

By mid-July, the WVS, with the full support of the Council, was into an 'Aluminium Drive', collected and guarded at a central dump adjoining the Council Offices. All receptacles contributed were punctured to ensure that they could be of no further domestic use but devoted entirely to the war effort. The WVS was hoping to secure 20,000 aluminium articles altogether. At this point, interesting items already contributed were a wheel, partly aluminium, which was part of the machinery of a Comet[11] (given by an officer of the RAF) and aluminium curtain rods from a local store-keeper. Some very valuable articles were handed in, many of which were new. In August 1940, the Council stressed the importance of an Order by the Minister of Home Security for the clearing of attics to minimise the risk of fire from incendiary bombs.

The collection of salvage continued, with spasmodic campaigns and exhortation to do better, as happened with 'Waste for the Pig'. These efforts were not always free from complications, as in March 1941 when tin was a problem. A large heap of tins had resulted from several months of collection and was destined for the furnaces of Lancashire. The problem was that the tins needed to be flattened. A trial scheme of doing this by steam-roller had obtained 18 tons of the metal from 100,000 tins. At this rate, the cost to the Council seemed likely to be about £1 per ton and it was clear that this could have been greatly reduced if the tins had been flattened before collection!

A special appeal went out from the Ministry of Supply in 1942 to increase the salvage of bones as the reduction in shipping meant that we were dependent upon home supply for making bone-meal fertiliser. It was recognised that this was a particularly difficult commodity to salvage as it depended on the provision of suitable receptacles and prompt collection if it was not to become offensive.

Another scheme which caught the public eye was the 'Mile of Books' organised by the Girl Guides. In the first week this reached more than half-way. About the same time, in July 1942, Daisy Gray and her team of helpers caused a stir by driving a loud-speaker car round the town appealing for salvage of all kinds. A little boy called Brian Smith walked into the Council Offices

---

[11] de Havilland DH 88 Comet, twin-engine racing monoplane

with 3,000 milk-bottle tops (the cardboard kind) and three months later, another named Tony Gunn achieved similar notoriety. From the oldest to the youngest, the residents were involved in collecting paper, rags, carpets, bones or anything that could possibly help win the war.

Among the compulsory measures was a survey of railings, iron and steel posts, chains, bollards and gates to be carried out by the Council in the autumn of 1941. Owners had 14 days in which to lodge an appeal, but the Ministry of Supply hoped that the majority would surrender such things freely and keep claims for compensation to a minimum. Within the next six to eight weeks, the appearance of the locality must have changed considerably as the Ministry of Works and Buildings removed what they needed. In October 1942, Hatfield took fourth place in the Rural District Division of the National Waste Paper Contest, collecting 12.3 tons per 1,000 population. The disposal of the £250 prize money was at the Council's discretion and it seems in keeping with the attitude of the locality that it was subsequently resolved to contribute that sum to the Red Cross Prisoner of War Fund.

**Presentation of a plaque to HMS *Tweed* by the
4th Marquess of Salisbury (see Chapter 7)**

THIS attitude was also clearly reflected in the town's response to other challenging appeals. No one could accuse Hatfield of being laggardly or unpatriotic. As well as all the usual charities, plus some extra wartime ones, and all the salvage demands, there were national efforts in which Hatfield was determined to play as great a part as any of its neighbours.

In August 1940, as the 'Battle of Britain' began in earnest, the Council launched the Hatfield Spitfire Fund in an effort to raise £5,000. An auxiliary fund was set up in Northaw and Cuffley, and details of progress included accounts of individuals such as the six-year-old evacuee who gave 6d pocket money. There was a barometer outside the Council Offices in St Albans Road to indicate how things were going and a record of subscribers' names inside the Office. By late September, Mr Denchfield of Stockbreach Road had made a model of a Spitfire diving towards a crashed Messerschmitt and this had been presented to the Council for the Fund. Mr Boon had raised £1 10s 6d from the sale of a sack of potatoes and school children were eagerly ordering Spitfire brooches which had already raised £5 at St Audrey's School. Towards the end of the year, more support was urged as the total had reached only £1,300. The fund eventually closed in May 1941 having achieved a total of £1,684 8s 2d. Whilst this represented approximately one-third of the ambitious original target, it was seen as a 'splendid effort' having regard to the many other calls on the community.

By that time one splendid effort had been superseded by another. In April 1941, the Council put a great deal of planning

45

into the National Savings Campaign 'War Weapons Week' to start on 19 April. The opening ceremony at the Council Offices was addressed by Lord Salisbury. On the Sunday, a procession of 600 led by the band of the Duke of Cornwall's Light Infantry, followed by detachments of the military and the Air Force, Home Guard, Civil Defence, nurses, police, ARP Wardens, Guides and Scouts marched through the streets to the Athletic Ground in Stonecross Road for a drumhead service conducted by the Dean of St Albans. The Chairman of the War Weapons Week Committee (Westminster Bank Manager, Mr Wright) read a letter from the Chancellor of the Exchequer encouraging Hatfield to do its best. Wednesday evening saw a concert in the Public Hall, followed on Thursday by a Cabaret Show.

Throughout the week an exhibition focusing on the Air Force and the products of local factories was displayed in the Recreation Room, Newtown, with a captured Messerschmitt which attracted large crowds. Perhaps the most topical attraction of the whole week was one entitled 'Hitting the Nail in Hitler's Coffin'. All this activity and excitement was directed towards a target of £50,000. By the time it was reported in the local press, £87,000 had been raised and the total subsequently soared to £91,000 before closing at the phenomenal total of £149,045 3s 6d.

In February 1942, another tremendous effort was called for when Hatfield and District set out to raise £120,000 to provide the navy with a fully-equipped corvette. 'Warship Week' was planned for the second week in March. Much interest was stimulated in the National Savings Movement and small investors were encouraged to save regularly. The opening ceremony was again addressed by Lord Salisbury at the Council Offices and, on the same Saturday evening, a dance was held in the Public Hall. Sunday's church parade was under the direction of Major Bishop and the salute was taken by Lord Salisbury followed by a service in the parish church. A concert arranged by the St John's Ambulance Service also took place on the Sunday at the Regent Cinema. The week continued with concerts, film shows and dances, ending on Saturday night with a dance at the Stonehouse Hotel arranged by the ARP.

The District also rallied, with Cuffley aiming at £20,000 and Essendon £14,500. North Mymms advertised 'the greatest whist drive in living memory!' With the final total still undeclared, the Council formally adopted HMS *Tweed* at the end of April 1942. At the presentation ceremony, held in St Audrey's School playground the following week, it emerged that the town had in fact adopted a frigate instead of a corvette as originally planned. The Admiral, on receiving the plaque made from oak grown in Hatfield Park from Lord Salisbury, said it would probably be placed on the quarterdeck of HMS *Tweed*, one of the war's latest and most up-to-date vessels. The sum, in excess of £150,000, which had been raised by Hatfield and District had provided for a ship already at sea and involved in the dangerous task of protecting convoys, a task in which she was already proving to be invaluable.

By January 1944, Mr Wright was encouraging residents to 'adopt' a sailor on board HMS *Tweed* and to write to him, but this plan was sadly aborted when in the early days of February the ship was lost. The Council discussed the possibility of taking steps towards its replacement. Eighty-three hands had gone down with the ship but those who survived had resolved to carry out the wishes of their comrades and pass on any remaining 'canteen funds' to Hatfield Hospital. As there was no local hospital, it was suggested that the money should go either to the Hatfield Nursing Association or to form the nucleus of a fund to build a hospital for the town after the war. The surviving senior officer, Lieut. Commander Stevenson Miller, was to be consulted on this matter.

A communication by pigeon-post in March 1943 marked the onset of yet another National Savings campaign. The message sent by Lord Kindersley from Trafalgar Square reached the Hatfield Savings Committee as they were on the brink of announcing their target for the 'Wings for Victory Week' which was to be at the end of May. The aim was to attract sufficient funds during that week to be able to purchase seven Mosquito bombers for the RAF, so it was not surprising to find the slogan coined as 'A Mosquito a Day'. Hatfield and District aimed to raise £20,000 more than their target in Warship Week the previous year which had been so outstandingly successful in raising £153,460 11s 0d. The £140,000 required for the Mosquitoes was in fact reached within the first four days and the target was increased to £200,000. This would enable them to put ten Mosquitoes instead of seven into the coming 'Battle for Europe'.

'Wings for Victory Week' was planned to include many of the most successful events from the previous annual campaigns. In his opening address on Saturday 22 May, Lord Salisbury stressed Hatfield's particular links with—and pride in—the air services and urged ordinary people to an even greater effort than in earlier years. He went on to open a special exhibition of aeroplanes and aeroplane parts while Geoffrey de Havilland in a Mosquito entertained the crowd with a low-flying air display. Targets were set for local schools and industries, and achievements were recorded on a 'novel indicator in the station yard' which showed enemy aircraft factories bombed by Mosquitoes every time Hatfield's total went up.

The usual procession took place on Sunday with a drumhead service in Hatfield Park followed throughout the week by film displays, dances, concerts and ultimately a fête and children's sports afternoon in the Recreation Ground. This had been the venue on Wednesday for an evening of community singing accompanied by the Home Guard Band. One of the week's sporting events was a football match between St Audrey's School and the de Havilland Ladies' team. The report of the match omitted to give the score though it stressed that no quarter was asked or given. The theme of the week was underlined by daily displays of gliding at de Havilland's. By the beginning of June, a total of £294,000 had been raised, more than double the original target. The town's success can be seen more clearly by comparing this total with a reported figure of £655,000 for the City of St Albans.

The National Savings Campaign in May 1944 was entitled 'Salute the Soldier Week' and its target was double the original 'Wings for Victory' target. Of this, £140,000 was to be set aside to replace HMS *Tweed*. When the final total of £327,792 was announced, it was stated that Hatfield had 'flashed past the winning post.'

The community spirit that grew out of these campaigns is illustrated in the following account of the 'Holidays at Home' project which was held between 29 July and 8 August 1944. The resident population and staff from the various military units stationed in the district worked together to provide all age groups with a range of attractions and events which could not be rivalled today. Five dances to suit all tastes were held in the Public Hall with music provided by local bands such as Sid Rumbelow's and Billie Hill's. There were Concerts and Concert Parties in the Public Hall and also in the Riding School with troops from RAF Mill Green and ENSA[12] taking part. Sports events included a comic Cricket Match and a Table Tennis Tournament, while Stonecross Road was the venue for the somewhat unusual sight of a Baseball Match and Boxing Display. The Baseball teams came from the US Forces General Hospital, North Mymms, and the boxers were from the RAF and US Forces, although civilian boxers were also invited.

Punch and Judy Shows took place at different venues throughout the District each day and three Hiking Tours were arranged and led by Mr Cyril Panter. The longest of these was a whole day hike covering 16 miles.

On Bank Holiday Monday, there was the Horticultural Show in the Public Hall and a Gala Event on the North Front in Hatfield Park with Sideshows, a Baby Show, Children's and Adult Sports Events, and Beauty Competitions for men and women—the

---

[12] ENSA: Entertainments National Service Association, set up in 1939 to provide entertainment for British armed forces personnel

Ladies' prize being a voucher for £2 2s 0d and the Men's prize free haircuts for a year. The Regent Cinema had the 'super attraction' of *Happy Go Lucky* starring Dick Powell and Mary Martin and *Let George Do It* featuring George Formby. Various competitions were held, one of which admirably captures the mood of the time. This was a 'Make Do and Mend' competition, organised by the Women's Institute, with prizes for different classes, such as:

- Best Meatless Dish
- Best Attractive Sweet (to include dried egg and dried milk)
- Best Child's Garment (from material previously used)

It is interesting to note that the programme of events included an appeal for Voluntary Farm Workers willing to give their services for the week to local farmers to assist with the harvest. They were encouraged to take this 'opportunity for healthy recreation and at the same time contribute materially to gathering in the country's food supply or to the essential farm work.'

By this stage of the war, an air of optimism was beginning to be felt, but this had to be tempered with caution as German V1 Flying Bombs had recently started to threaten our towns. In view of this, it is not surprising that the programme contained a section listing the conveniently sited ARP Shelters at the following points:

- Great North Road (near Men's Social Club)
- Great North Road (Gray's Garage)
- French Horn Lane (opposite West Goldings)
- Beaconsfield Road
- St Albans Road (near Regent Cinema)
- Roe Green
- Wellfield Road

There was also special mention of the Warden's Post adjoining the Westminster Bank in the Great North Road. Thankfully no incidents were recorded during this period, which would have disrupted events and deprived the public of this opportunity for enjoyment and relaxation.

Chapter 8   The Workers

IT is quite apparent that by the outbreak of war this small town of the early 1930s had begun to change very rapidly under the combined pressures of industrial growth and the demands of the nation. As the size of the work-force employed in the district increased, so did the range of trades and skills involved. By now, de Havilland's was the major employer in the town with hundreds of engineers, sheet metal workers, electricians, vehicle builders, painters, woodworkers and furniture trade workers, each group being represented by its own union. There were powerful voices to be heard including those of the Communists among the de Havilland shop stewards, and they were not slow in their attempts to influence local affairs. The arrival of other industrial concerns, such as Jack Olding and Co. Ltd at about that time provided the work-force of Hatfield with a further boost to its numbers and importance.

The workers employed at de Havilland's in particular could not possibly all be housed in the town and from the early years many travelled out daily from North London. There was constant and increasing pressure for more local housing to supplement the building that had taken place in the Garden Village, Birchwood and Selwyn areas in the 1930s. However, this could not be seriously considered during the war years when it was all the authorities could do to deal with the repairs and possible reconstruction of bombed buildings.

Among the measures taken to cope with this ever expanding work-force was the setting up of a hostel for female workers from de Havilland's at Ayot House, Ayot St Lawrence, and another for the factory's male workers in Alma Road, St Albans. In 1941, active consideration was being given to the opening of a Communal Feeding Centre in the town to provide meals for school children, to serve the needs of the further influx of workers and also to be available to cope with emergency situations. The two sites eventually selected for this purpose were the Carmelite Convent in Batterdale in the old town and the Salvation Army Mission Hall at the rear of the White Lion in St Albans Road. In 1943, by which time the centres had been designated as The British Restaurant, it was reported that the Salvation Army Hall was averaging 250 meals per day (with up to 60 people seated at one time) and their peak demand had been 327 meals in one day.

It was of course essential to have adequate transport services available, particularly the railway, to ensure that the workers and supplies could get to the factories. At the beginning of the war, there was a considerable increase in goods being carried by rail and the passenger service was run on an emergency timetable. At one point in the autumn of 1939, the passenger service from Hatfield to St Albans was suspended but, in December 1939, a limited passenger service was restored for the workers at the de Havilland factory and was clearly tailored to fit working-hours at the factory. A public timetable for December of that year shows passenger trains leaving St Albans Abbey Station for Hatfield at 7.45 a.m., 1.40 p.m. (Sat. only), 4.15 p.m. and 5.35 p.m. At first, the workers travelled either to Nast Hyde Halt or to Hatfield (main line) but, in 1942, Lemsford Road Halt was opened alongside the bridge which spanned the St Albans Road. From there, it was a short walk to the factory gate. It was hoped that by improving the convenience of the rail journey, fewer cars would be brought to the factory, thus saving scarce fuel. The Lemsford Road Halt did not appear in the public railway timetables and was unstaffed although a porter travelled from Hatfield from time to time to collect tickets. To encourage the use of the railway, a workman's ticket was made cheaper than the bus fare, but it is not clear if this device had any positive effect.

After the opening of the Halt in August 1942, an early morning train was extended from Hatfield to the Halt. After unloading, the train backed down the line to Hatfield. In the evening, the empty train was backed to the Halt from Hatfield and, after picking up its passengers, it proceeded via Hatfield to King's Cross. When Hill End Hospital became a military hospital, with Bart's evacuated there from London, the line was invaluable for hospital trains and to supply the hospital with fuel and other commodities.

Vehicles parked at de Havilland as obstacles against enemy landings

Much has been written elsewhere about the role of the de Havilland Aircraft Co. during the war. Its very existence made Hatfield a target for enemy air attack, particularly during 1940 when a number of bombs fell in the vicinity—though the factory experienced only one direct hit (described in Chapter 9). The secrecy over the Lemsford Road Halt was, in all probability, intended to avoid attracting attention to the neighbourhood. A more positive attempt to divert attention was the establishment of a decoy airfield, complete with dummy aircraft, at Panshanger.

We now look back and see the de Havilland factory's wartime role as being dominated by the production of the Mosquito.

Its value in this connection cannot be over-stressed but it should not be forgotten that the factory also made other valuable contributions to the war effort.

At the beginning of the war, Tiger Moth[13] production was under way and these aircraft were to become important in the training of pilots for the RAF in the early days of the war. The Tiger Moths were the mainstay of No. 1 Elementary Flying Training School stationed at the south end of the aerodrome, administered by the RAF but maintained and serviced by local civilian workers. Repairs and refitting of Hurricanes and Spitfires were undertaken at Hatfield and, in later years, development work was taking place on the site for new aircraft such as the Hornet[14] and the Vampire[15].

Home Guard Company on parade at Jack Olding's Factory, 1942

Another local company heavily involved in the war effort was Jack Olding & Co. Ltd. The firm had moved to Hatfield a few months before the outbreak of war and occupied prestigious new

---

[13] de Havilland DH 82 Tiger Moth, two-seat primary trainer
[14] de Havilland DH 103 Hornet, twin-engine fighter
[15] de Havilland DH 100 Vampire, twin-boom jet fighter

premises at the junction of Great North Road and the Barnet By-Pass (the site of the present Tesco Store). Jack Olding, an ebullient, extrovert, self-made businessman had acquired the rights for the servicing and distribution of US earth-moving equipment produced by Caterpillar, John Deere and La Plante Chaote to most parts of the UK. Far-sighted though he may have been, it is difficult to believe that he could have envisaged that, within such a short while, his workers would be so deeply immersed in supporting the vital war effort.

The demand for such equipment grew rapidly as the war progressed and the Company acquired a Ministry of Defence contract for the servicing and modification of both British-built Churchill tanks and Sherman and Grant tanks imported from North America. The expanded civilian workforce was also supplemented by military personnel (Royal Engineers in particular) who were sent to the works to be trained in operating and maintaining the tanks and other machinery. Some of those who worked at the factory at the time retain happy memories of the concert parties held in the canteen at lunchtimes and the keep-fit classes run by Eileen Fowler. Much of the work of testing the tanks and earth-moving equipment was carried out alongside the Hertford Road at Mill Green (now the site of a golf course) on land owned by Lord Salisbury. Accommodation for the soldiers on training courses was provided initially in the homes of local residents but, in due course, huts were erected in a field adjacent to the factory for this purpose.

The Vauxhall factory at Luton was also involved in work on tanks at this time, and reports indicate that large numbers of tanks were brought from Luton on the Hatfield, Luton and Dunstable railway to Ayot before being transported by road to Hatfield for testing.

Closely allied to the activities at Jack Olding's works was the RAF Camp at Mill Green. The Camp was set up in 1942 and became the home of No. 2 School of Aircraft Construction and also a Plant Depot for No. 5201 Plant Squadron. Anecdotes from some of the airmen arriving there in the autumn of 1942 point to the fact that it had been set up in considerable haste. They relate that the site was a sea of mud and that the huts, situated in the wooded areas, were barely habitable with minimal furniture and bedding and with the concrete floors still damp.

It was therefore with considerable reluctance that the men entered their new quarters but, like the rest of the population in those days, they were not daunted by adversity. Their stories tell how they quickly adjusted to their new surroundings and it was not long before they were regulars at the Welwyn Garden City pubs, particularly the Beehive, the Woodman and the Cherry Tree. Among their most lasting recollections are their evening visits to their favourite hostelries dressed in their best blues but having to carry their shoes while wearing wellington boots until they were well clear of the quagmire that was their camp. Once they reached the firm surface of the road, they would change into their shoes and find a suitable spot in the hedge where they could hide their wellingtons until their return. After a few pints, the task of finding a pair of wellingtons on a dark night must have been something of a game of chance and it is quite conceivable that the remains of a few RAF-issue wellingtons are still lying deep in the hedges along Ascots Lane.

Chapter 9   The de Havilland Bomb

BY the late summer of 1940, France had fallen and the Battle of Britain was raging in the skies over South East England. The first bomb to be dropped in the Hatfield District was recorded at Cuffley on 28 August without causing any casualties. There were several further incidents, fortunately without casualties or serious damage, throughout the month of September culminating with three high-explosive bombs at Hawkshead House near the Barnet By-Pass, south of Hatfield and several others at Cromer Hyde on 29 September. October began with a series of bombs including a high-explosive bomb at Coleman Green and some incendiary bombs which caused a fire but no casualties at Cook's Box Factory in Green Lanes. Many of the locals felt that it was only a matter of time before the enemy would be successful in striking their real target in the area. The prophets did not have long to wait as, on the morning of 3 October 1940, a Junkers Ju 88 dropped its bombs on the de Havilland factory and the residents of Hatfield knew that the war had reached their doorstep.

There are numerous eye-witness accounts of the raid, including several published in Alexander McKee's book, *The Mosquito Log*. The accounts contain certain variations, which is hardly surprising in view of the passage of time that has elapsed, but most of the important details recalled remain constant. Further research, subsequently undertaken by Terry Pankhurst, has provided additional vivid recollections of the events of that October morning and these are described in his book *When The Bombs Dropped*. There is no doubt that it was a very dull and misty morning, so there was no flying from the airfield at the time. The

German aircraft is reported to have originally set out on a mission to bomb an aerodrome at Reading (probably at Woodley). The navigator was on his first flight over England and with visibility so poor it proved impossible to identify the intended target. Seeking an alternative target, the aircraft turned eastwards and, despite low cloud, the pilot identified aircraft on the ground as he approached Hatfield. Several eye-witnesses saw an aircraft heading towards the airfield at a very low level and assumed that it was British. Having made one pass over the factory, the pilot veered off on a right-hand circuit returning from the south-east a few minutes later and dropped a stick of four bombs which landed on the grass and bounced into one of the factory workshops (the '94 shop').

The wrecked '94 shop' after the Junkers Ju 88 dropped its bombs

As the aircraft passed over on its second circuit, it was fired at and hit by the Light Anti-Aircraft Battery stationed at the aerodrome, while the crew of the attacking aircraft returned fire.

Eye-witnesses recall that, prior to the bombs exploding, bullets were bouncing off the roof of the flying school parachute room, sounding like ping pong balls. Another unconfirmed report states that the shots which damaged the aircraft were from a Bofors gun of 145 Battery of the Light Anti-Aircraft Regiment, commanded by Col (later Sir) Mortimer Wheeler. Other local units, including a battery located at Briars Lane, made similar claims. It is, in fact, likely that more than one unit struck crippling blows.

Having dropped its bombs, the Junkers headed off eastwards towards Hertford with flames trailing from its starboard engine. In an attempt to gain height, the crew ejected their machine guns, helmets and other equipment over the countryside but it was to no avail and the aircraft crash-landed in flames at East End Green Farm, near Cole Green at 11.40 a.m. Other reliable sources have suggested that the raid took place somewhat earlier than previously reported and that the

Soldier guarding the Junkers Ju 88

aircraft crashed soon after 11 o'clock. The pilot, Oberleutnant Siegward Fiebig and his three crew members, Oberfeldwebel Erich Goebel, Feldwebel Heinz Ruthof and Unteroffizier Kurt Seifert all managed to get out of the burning machine before it was totally engulfed in flames, and were arrested unhurt. Two were taken to Hertford Police Station while the pilot and fourth member of the crew were taken to Hatfield Police Station and subsequently transferred to Canada as Prisoners of War.

The devastation at the factory was considerable with the '94 shop' completely burnt out and with widespread blast damage to many of the nearby buildings. Twenty-one workers lost their lives, six of whom were buried in a combined grave in St Luke's churchyard where their plot is marked with an appropriate memorial stone. There were some seventy other casualties, most of whom were taken for treatment at Hill End Hospital with others going to Hertford County Hospital or to the military hospital at Hatfield House. Basic air-raid precautions had been installed at the works including a look-out post on the top of the factory which was manned at all times. However, in such weather conditions, it would have been extremely difficult to identify an enemy aircraft until it was close.

Therefore, the klaxon was sounded only a short while before the bombs were dropped. Various dug-out shelters had been built within the grounds and other rather crude shelters, made in the form of single-brick walls supporting concrete roofs, had been erected inside the factory. These proved totally inadequate in these circumstances and the collapsed roofs contributed to the death toll.

A local resident who was working in the '94 shop' at the time describes how he had his tools spread out around him when a panic-stricken voice over the Tannoy rang out with the message, 'Take cover!' He was standing alongside a partition on the other side of which was an indoor shelter. For some inexplicable reason, he did not run towards the shelter but in the opposite direction to the opening at the other end of the shop. He was carrying his gas mask in its wooden case when the blast hurled him through the opening. He found himself wedged between the wall of the '94 shop' and the rubble from a collapsed hangar. He was able to crawl through a gap and fortunately was unhurt. As he got to his feet, firemen were hurrying past so he joined the fire crew and helped them put out fires among the rubble. He continued to help with the rescue work until about 2 p.m. when he decided it was time to go home for something to eat. On arrival he found his wife in a very distressed state as she had been informed by a Company representative that he had been posted as missing. He was back at work the following morning but all his tools had been lost.

There is a story told by a number of local residents that the pilot of the Junkers Ju 88 had been a student at de Havilland's before the war and that his first flight over the factory had been a warning to the workers before he was forced to obey orders and drop his bombs. This story has been strongly denied by those who would have been his contemporaries including John Cunningham, later to become the Company's Chief Test Pilot. One thing that is not in doubt among those who witnessed the raid is the skill and courage of the German pilot and crew in carrying out their mission in such difficult flying conditions. This acknowledgement can be made after the passage of time but naturally had no place in the thoughts of British people in those dark days.

The effects of the raid on production cannot be overestimated but the disaster could have been so much greater. It must be remembered that, by that time, the prototype Mosquito (DH 98) was at an advanced stage of its development amid great secrecy at Salisbury Hall, and it was only one month later, on 3 November 1940, that the first Mosquito left Salisbury Hall by road for Hatfield where it first took to the air on 25 November 1940.

From this period onwards, a large section of the Hatfield workforce spent the remainder of the war years engaged on Mosquito production. The story of the Mosquito became one of the great success stories of the war and is still viewed with pride by local residents.

Inevitably, triumphs of this scale are never achieved without the occasional setback and human tragedy. One such incident, which shocked and saddened the community and was a great personal blow to the de Havilland family, and the whole factory, took place on the afternoon of Monday, 23 August 1943. Two Mosquito aircraft on test flights collided in mid-air over open ground near

Oaklands, between the airfield and St Albans, killing the four crew. They were the two test pilots John de Havilland (24) of Bushey Heath, George Gibbins (34) of St Albans, Godfrey Carter (32) of Welwyn who was a supervisor in the flight shed, and John Scrope (24) of Hatfield, a member of the Aero Dynamics Department, all highly valued employees of the Company. It was estimated that the planes were flying at approximately 600 feet when one banked sharply and struck the left-hand side of the other near the wing. Eye-witnesses told the inquest of a terrible explosion and fragments falling in all directions. The parachutist seen descending must have been John de Havilland who died on the way to hospital. The other three victims were found among the wreckage, not having had time to eject.

The importance of the de Havilland factory to the war effort is very clear but one should not overlook the vital contribution made by other large and small factories, workshops and even homes in the surrounding towns and villages, where components were manufactured and assembled. The value of having a dispersed workforce became quite apparent after the events of 3 October 1940. Furthermore, as production increased, it was a means of utilising accommodation and resources where they were available and enabled more women to make a direct contribution to the war effort.

Life was hard for everyone in the war years—service personnel and civilians alike—but there was thankfully still time to enjoy the lighter moments of pranks and practical jokes in the workplace. An example of this is related by a former de Havilland worker recalling the arrival of female workers to undertake welding work alongside male colleagues. He clearly remembers that when the girls left their bench for any reason the lads would fill their goggles with soot so that when they replaced them they looked like minstrels. The girls quickly learned to retaliate by putting lipstick on the lads' goggles which soon became smeared over their foreheads and cheeks.

THROUGHOUT the autumn of 1940 until the end of January 1941, over seventy separate bombing incidents involving incendiary or high explosive bombs were recorded in the Hatfield Rural District. Fortunately most of these incidents were in the less populated areas on open land near the surrounding villages. However, some high explosive bombs fell closer to the town, near Stockbreach Road, near the Council Offices and on the Poplars Estate during this period causing some structural damage but with no casualties. The de Havilland bombing had been quite shattering for the people of Hatfield but it is apparent that the devastation could have been so much worse.

It is not surprising in the circumstances that there was now renewed local pressure for the provision of shelters. The concern of the ARP and Shop Stewards Committee of de Havilland's about this had already been expressed, just before the bombing of the factory, at a meeting in the Public Hall addressed by Professor J B S Haldane. He was known nationally for his support of a policy of deep-shelter protection for workers and civilians alike. His recommendation of two-stage protection for factory workers which would begin as blast and splinter-proof and later be improved so that they would be bomb-proof was clearly too late for the twenty-one men who had lost their lives just a week earlier. Their colleagues were determined to press on and formed the Tenants' Defence League to persuade the District Council to act. Led by Harold Lydall, they obtained representation at a special meeting of the Council where they presented a 2,000 signature petition. The Council however was not able to respond as they wished as there was obviously a shortage of materials and money. The best that could be done was the construction of blast-walls and some shelters, such as the one at the Recreation Ground on St Albans Road. This clearly was not satisfactory to the workers who held an exhibition in January 1941 to demonstrate how inadequate the existing shelters were and what was really required in the way of reinforced concrete and bomb-proofing.

The League demanded a survey of the higher ground in the Old Town and Park for the purpose of excavating tunnels to be fitted with beds and air-conditioning. If tunnels were considered impractical then 'Haldane' shelters must be built for all residents not only of the Old Town, but also in Birchwood, the Garden Village, Bramble Road, Brookmans Park, Little Heath, North Mymms, Cuffley and the rest of the rural area. It is hardly surprising that little could be done to meet their demands.

The concern remained and, in April 1942, two possible schemes were discussed by the Council in order to provide adequate shelter for all the residents. It was decided to implement the larger-scale plan providing for the construction of sixty-five shelters for the accommodation of more than 2,500 people at a cost of some £10,000 plus, with the cost to be borne by the government. At the same meeting, disappointment was expressed that relatively few families had applied for Morrison table-shelters. A year later, it seemed that so many of those shelters were being used as work benches outside the houses of the occupants they were designed to protect that officials expressed the view that 'they might as well be collected as scrap metal!' It was not until August 1944 that it was reported to the Council that Anderson shelters could now be supplied for erection in residents' gardens.

The workers also involved themselves in local affairs in other ways. From March 1942, Hatfield had its own 'Trades Council', as distinct from its predecessor which had covered Welwyn Garden City as well. This group met regularly and engaged in active politics, seeking to influence the decisions of the District Council. One of their particular concerns was the contribution women were able to make to the war effort and one of their successes was the provision of nursery care to enable more women to go out to work.

Just before Christmas 1941, a local mother had been fined 15s for failing to send her seven-year-old daughter to school. The child was left in charge of two smaller children while the mother went off to work at de Havilland's and the three children had been found one day wandering along the Barnet By-Pass. It was this kind of situation that the new Birchwood Nursery was designed to prevent. The opening of the nursery hit the headlines as the first of its kind in the County. Although there were some doubts expressed about the educational value of leaving such young children in communal care all day, there is no doubt about the support the scheme gave to the war effort and the facility appears to have been well used from the outset. The workers were pressing, at about that time, for Play Centres as well and these Centres were opened at Newtown and Green Lanes Schools to enable children who needed to stay after school to have their tea there.

Local politics were also much concerned with food and the adequate and fair distribution of what supplies were available. The battle to appoint a Trades Council representative to the local Food Control Committee was protracted, involving at times both the TUC and the Ministry of Food. Ultimately, at the end of 1942, the District Council was forced to accept, under protest, one of the Trades Council nominees, David Shade. The Food Control Committee did not have an easy time, responsible as it was for supervising supplies and rationing as well as arrangements for communal feeding. An example of the conflicts that arose is a row that broke out in September 1941 over the storage of eggs until they went bad. The view was expressed that it would have been better not to ration eggs but to encourage everyone to keep chickens.

At their next meeting eight months later, however, it was stated that it had not been necessary to call members of the Food Control Committee together until then because of 'the excellent and smooth work of the food organisation in this district.' Warm appreciation was expressed for all the work put in by Mr Morgan and his staff. There was some discussion of the 'points' system which seemed to be causing shopkeepers a great deal of extra work, and housewives were urged to study the system a little more and assist grocers in particular by being more specific in their orders and not just sending their ration books in with requests for 'goods on points'.

There had been a small improvement in the numbers of qualified staff in the retail trade (according to a communication from the Divisional Food Officer) and the overcrowding in the Food Office had been recognised by the Ministry of Works. Additional premises were being acquired at the corner of Ground Lane and this would make it possible to provide a better service to the public.

Shopkeepers had problems over and above those of ordinary citizens in wartime. Householders had to ensure that the black-out regulations were strictly observed and ran the risk of prosecution if they failed to do so. In addition to these restrictions, shopkeepers found that their opening hours were curtailed with the rather liberal pre-war closing times cut back by at least an hour. They also fought hard against the abolition of lunch-hour closing, introduced to enable more people to do their shopping in daylight hours. Traders tried to provide for emergencies which could occur at any time by making 'Mutual Assistance Pacts' so that:

> In the event of the premises of one trader being damaged in an air raid, other members of the same trade in the district would combine to supply such goods and assistance as might be necessary to enable the affected business to continue to supply its customers.

In June 1940, Mr Joe Walby outlined the arrangements made by the local butchers as an example to other groups of traders and added:

> Two years ago, I would not have believed that any body of traders could, and would, work together as the butchers of Hatfield are doing now.

Concern was also expressed about the using up of scarce petrol (not to mention staff time) in making deliveries to outlying customers. Mr A A Dollimore suggested a scheme by which traders could co-operate so that perhaps as many as six different deliveries to one house could be made by the same van. Clearly such a scheme would require a considerable amount of organisation and there is no evidence that it was ever seriously pursued although, in June 1942, arrangements were made for the rationalisation of milk deliveries.

In March 1942, a further policy of mutual aid was adopted, this time by the non-food traders. The objectives of the Mutual Assistance Committee were to ensure minimum disruption to trade, safeguard essential supplies to the public, protect and salvage stock, and market new stocks arriving in the town quickly. An illustration of the way in which traders had to make the best possible use of the limited supplies they were able to obtain is shown in a local press report dated July 1943. On that occasion a well-respected shopkeeper, Mr Eric Tingey, was summoned to court for refusing to sell cups with handles unless the customer also bought a cup without a handle. The case was dismissed when it was explained that in March the firm had received a delivery of 33 dozen cups with handles and another 10 dozen without and that they were trying to distribute the stock fairly!

The presence of service personnel in and around the town produced benefits for some of the traders in that it helped secure regular supplies to satisfy their military contracts. A local shoe repairer recalls that, having the contract to repair the footwear of the soldiers based in Hatfield Park, he could be fairly sure of a regular supply of leather and other essential materials. It is apparent that a considerable amount of mutual goodwill built up among the traders of Hatfield but, despite all their efforts, they knew that it might still be insufficient in an emergency. In view of this they felt it necessary to pass a resolution that the Regional Commissioner should be empowered to requisition suitable property in order to safeguard stock for which there was no accommodation.

The members of the new Hatfield Trades Council were active, raising a wide range of local issues in need of attention. While battling to get representation on the Food Control Committee, they were tackling the local authority about such issues as the poor state of several footpaths in Hatfield, the safety of the new Lemsford Road Halt in black-out conditions and complaints about neglect of salvage collection in some parts of the district. Their particular concern about travelling facilities was raised at an Area Transport Conference at Luton in the autumn of 1942 but it is not known how effective their pressure for action on these and other issues proved to be.

Look-out Post on the 'South Front' at Hatfield House

Chapter 11 Involvement at Home and Abroad

FOLLOWING the German invasion of the USSR in June 1941, the Communist Party, well represented at the de Havilland factory, changed its stance from one of disagreeing with the war to active support. At the beginning of 1942, they began a series of communications with prominent figures on the world stage by sending a declaration to Churchill. It was signed by almost 1,000 workers and congratulated him on his efforts for the country, at the same time urging him to remove from the Government anyone with pro-Nazi sympathies and promising renewed efforts to increase their production for the war. On the anniversary of the Anglo–Soviet Pact, a further message sent to the Prime Minister called for the opening up of a second front in Europe and the end of the ban placed on the *Daily Worker* newspaper. Later recipients of telegrams from the de Havilland Shop Stewards' Committee were military leaders Eisenhower, Alexander and Montgomery (on the conquest of Tunisia), Alexander, and the Russian Embassy (on the conquest of Sicily and victory at Orel) and another to Churchill (on the surrender of Italy).

While their local pressure for improved transport, housing for workers, food and nurseries was maintained, the second front and, in 1943, the social-security developments envisaged in the Beveridge Report[16], received their vociferous support. At the same time, efforts were being made to provide sufficient funds to pay for a ward at Stalingrad Hospital. A committee, with Frank Clayton as secretary and Mr 'Daddy' Young as treasurer, asked the

---

[16] Beveridge Report: publ. 1942, influential in founding of Welfare State

District Council for permission to collect, in addition to the Aid for Russia flag-day. It proved to be a magnificent co-operative effort between groups of all political colours in Hatfield, achieving a target of £1,500 with the help of Lord Salisbury, president of the fund, the local MP, Sir Francis Fremantle, and the Rector of St Etheldreda's, who organised a dance to raise money for the fund. The official acknowledgement of this effort, which came from the Soviet Ambassador perhaps as late as 1946, stated:

> The Soviet people will never forget the help rendered to them by the British people during the hard years of the war against our common enemy.

This spirit of harmony between the workers and those in authority was not apparent on other major issues. For example, when Sir Francis Fremantle died soon after the Stalingrad Hospital Appeal, there was an attempt to set up a conference involving all four political parties to nominate his successor. This move had the support not only of the Trades Council and the de Havilland shop stewards, but also various unions, the Communist Party and the Cuffley Labour Party. The plan received short shrift from Lord Salisbury who reminded them of the Party truce in existence for the duration of the national emergency. A Conservative candidate was the only possible replacement and in the course of time the Hon. John Grimston became the local MP (unopposed).

Opposition to fascism, wherever it was found, was high on the workers' list of priorities and there was active resistance to the release of Oswald Mosley from prison in November 1943. Workers from de Havilland's demonstrated the extent of their colleagues' feelings by appearing in protest outside the Home Office. There was also a petition which circulated in Hatfield but such action bore no fruit.

Another issue close to the hearts of the workers was that of factory canteens. A committee was set up in March 1943 to run the canteens. The committee received the congratulations of Government Ministers for its efforts in sending a petition to Ernest Bevin and Stafford Cripps in support of Bevin's fight in the Canteen Bill against catering interests. The de Havilland factory received a visit from the Prime Minister in April 1943 and there is no doubt that the shop stewards took this opportunity to reinforce the strongly held views they had expressed previously in their telegrams to him.

The Hatfield Fire Brigade was another group whose operations extended beyond the immediate locality as they became involved in regional support to other parts as emergencies arose. In January 1941, with the Blitz raging in London and enemy air attacks on other cities such as Southampton and Manchester, fire services were stretched to their limits. The Clerk reported to the Rural District Council that Auxiliary Firemen Armstrong, Jefferies and Moore were sent to Manchester while Fireman Wicks took a mobile water-dam to London with emergency rations and blankets. A letter was also read from the Southampton Fire Brigade thanking the Hatfield men for assistance given under the regional scheme during and after severe air-raids. The letter referred to the devotion to duty and the promptness with which the Hatfield men carried out their instructions.

A similar report to the Parish Council described the excellence of the Fire Brigade and AFS since the outbreak of war. This spirit was exemplified in Fire Patrol Officer L J Stockley, a local member of the AFS who, in February 1941, volunteered to help a naval squad deal with an unexploded missile near houses at Cuffley. He was commended by the Regional Commissioner for the courage, enthusiasm and devotion to duty he displayed. As a reward, the Council decided to present a gratuity of £5 to the Officer at Cuffley Fire Station on 8 March.

Later in March, it was reported that the Hatfield AFS pump crew was fire-fighting in London during the Blitz of the previous week. They stayed overnight in the capital and were named as Section Officer Lovell, Fireman Howe and Auxiliary Firemen Moore, Hatch and Coleman.

Home Guard Battalions marching past the Hatfield War Memorial in the Great North Road

These additional wartime demands had to be undertaken while still being available to handle the inevitable local incidents, be it a fire at the rear of Peter's Café, a burned-out lorry on the Barnet By-Pass or the truck of lime which caught fire on the railway in August 1941. On that particular occasion, it took seven hours to extinguish the blaze and several firemen were left with blistered feet and wrists. Such fires would have presented problems in normal conditions but, with the fear of the light from fires attracting attacks from the air, the hazards were that much greater. In October 1941, the Council considered it appropriate to formally register its appreciation of the loyal, devoted and cheerful service readily rendered by all the Fire Brigade and AFS personnel over the previous three years. This appreciation marked the transfer of the service from local to national control and the Council felt sure that the same patriotic response would continue.

No account of the Second World War would be complete without mention of the Home Guard, formed throughout the country following a broadcast by the Secretary of State for War, Anthony Eden, on 14 May 1940, as the Dutch Army was on the point of surrender. Originally known as the LDV (Local Defence Volunteers), their title was soon changed to Home Guard in July 1940. Initially the only items of uniform issued to the men were a cap badge and an armlet but, in due course, full military uniforms were issued and in February 1941 matters were formalised by permitting the use of army ranks.

At the outset, Herts Zone comprised one battalion with twenty companies, within which Hatfield formed the No. 10 Company. Numbers grew rapidly and, by the end of 1940, Hertfordshire had re-grouped into ten battalions with thirty-five companies. The Hatfield unit formed the 10th Company of the 4th Battalion while de Havilland, Hatfield, became the 19th Company of the same battalion. Evidence suggests that these groups of volunteers were viewed with scepticism and were subject to ridicule in some quarters in the early days with stories of them patrolling the perimeter of the de Havilland airfield armed with only a broom-handle or pitchfork, or cycling through the lanes with a Sten gun strapped to the handle bars. This image changed as the threat of invasion grew and the value of all forms of defence gained credibility.

Further reorganisation of the local Home Guard units became necessary and, by the end of 1942, Hatfield was part of the Central Sector with 13th Battalion Headquarters at de Havilland's controlling Companies A, B, C & D, and an additional Light Anti-Aircraft Battery based at the factory and 14th Battalion Headquarters at North Place (Northcotts) on the Great North Road (in Old Hatfield) controlling four Companies, one at the Headquarters, one at Jack Olding's and the others at Essendon and Brookmans Park.

Records show that the Hatfield Town Company (14A) had responsibility for the security of strategic points around the district with platoons based at railway bridges—such as those at Ground Lane, Batterdale and The Wrestlers—as well as at other important locations including the Gas Works.

Personnel changed as the war progressed but, after the 1942 re-organisation, the Officers commanding the two local battalions were shown as 13th Battalion, Lt Col H J Allen, and 14th Battalion, Lt Col R N Greenwood MC. Their respective deputies were Maj. Butcher DSO and Maj. R W M Arbuthnot MC. The 14A Company was commanded by Maj. C F Randall with Capt. C J Hewson as second-in-command, both well-known local residents and veterans of the First World War.

A member of the local Scout Troop at the time and a lifelong resident of the town recalled that the Scout Master, 'Skip' Day, formed a unit of the Army Cadet Force from the senior members of the Scout Troop. They would meet regularly at Dellfield School for their training and went out on exercises with the local Home Guard either in Hatfield Park or on weekend camp further afield. It is interesting to speculate how the mature members of the Home Guard viewed this injection of youth into their ranks. No doubt they proved to be a mixed blessing, their exuberance proving difficult to control but their fresh legs bringing respite as the manoeuvres dragged on.

A fascinating insight into the activities and attitudes of some of the members of the Home Guard can be obtained from the diaries kept by one of them throughout the war. Randall Tingey spent his whole working life running the long-established family grocery business in the town, a task made considerably more difficult at that time by the loss of many of the experienced staff who had been called up for military service and the effects of rationing.

Despite these pressures Mr Tingey, like thousands of others, including his wife who had already become a volunteer with the Red Cross, felt a need to do something extra and therefore joined the local Home Guard. He described himself as 'very unwarlike' and would have been quite content to restrict his involvement to office-administration tasks, but this was not to be so. He soon learned that he would have to receive training and pass a test in Rifle Shooting, Field Craft, First Aid, Gas and General Knowledge. He resigned himself to this with the observation that whatever the result 'we shan't get the push.' In fact, when he subsequently was taken down to the rifle range behind Northcotts for the first time, he surprised himself by hitting the target with all five shots.

His diary also contains a detailed description of his preparations for the following morning's exercise as he spent the evening cleaning his boots, rolling his cape and packing his haversack. Then, at an early hour on a February Sunday morning, he reluctantly left 'the snug warmth of his bed' to go and man a field telephone in a bitterly cold cell under the Post Office. His assessment of the exercise was that it had been totally unsuccessful as his unit had failed to defend Hatfield for more than an hour! His comments on bayonet fighting-practice were expressed equally disparagingly as 'a very crude idea ... as if we were learning to fight redskins.'

He must have felt a sense of relief as he wrote his entry for 7 September 1944, to record the fact that there had been an unexpected announcement that compulsory Home Guard parades were to be discontinued in conjunction with the partial lifting of the black-out and reinstatement of restricted street lighting. Looking back on these events, it seems ironic that within a few weeks of these relaxations being introduced, the residents of Hatfield would suffer two of their most devastating and costly raids of the whole war.

Sherriff's Mill, Bull Stag Green. It was near here that Hatfield's first V1 flying bomb fell, Saturday, 24 June 1944. (see Chapter 12)

Chapter 12   The Selwyn Crescent Bomb

THE heavy bombing experienced from the autumn of 1940 to the spring of 1941, generally known as the Blitz, when the fear of invasion was at its height, could never be forgotten by those who had experienced it. However, as the war progressed, with allied successes overseas, the threat of attack from the air receded and raids became sporadic incidents throughout 1942 and 1943. This state of affairs was to change in the summer of 1944 with the arrival of a new more sinister terror, the V1 Flying Bomb, nicknamed the 'buzz bomb' or 'doodlebug'. By the autumn of 1944, we faced not only the dreaded V1 but also the even more destructive V2 Long Range Rocket, both of which were to rain down on our towns and cities from time to time until March 1945.

The first recorded Flying Bomb fell amid great confusion at Swanscombe, Kent, on 13 June 1944 and from then, until the last one fell at Datchworth on 29 March 1945, this part of the country was on a high state of alert. Within two weeks of the first V1, Hatfield had its first experience of this new weapon of destruction. Between 6.30 and 7.00 a.m. on the morning of Saturday 24 June, a Flying Bomb fell in a field near Sherriff's Mill alongside the railway line. If it had continued a few yards further west and exploded on the line, it would have caused major travel disruption on the mainline but thankfully the only damage was to property on this occasion. It proved to be the first of almost thirty V1 and V2 attacks recorded in the Hatfield Rural District, two of which were to involve the loss of lives and make heavy demands on the emergency services.

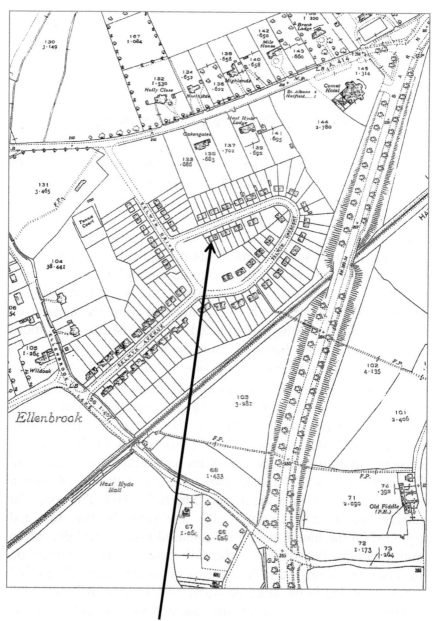

**V1 bomb fell here, demolishing Nos. 2 & 4 Selwyn
Crescent, killing four occupants**

Friday, 22 September 1944

78

The first of these serious bombings to have fatal consequences took place on Friday, 22 September 1944. It is interesting to link this attack with the bombing of the de Havilland factory almost four years earlier through the memories of Mr Jimmy Hall, a local resident, who experienced both raids at first hand.

Jimmy was a pupil of St Audrey's School at the outbreak of the war where he remembers digging trenches for shelters. Shortly after he obtained a job as a 'shop boy' at the de Havilland factory where his main responsibilities seemed to involve being at everyone's beck and call, cleaning down the work benches and writing out time-cards. He had been employed there for less than two months when the '94 shop' was bombed in October 1940 (see Chapter 9). He recalled how a section of fitters from his shop had that morning been moved in to '94'—it could so easily have been his section! As the klaxon sounded, one of the men made young Jimmy put on his tin hat and get under the bench until it was all over. When they eventually let him out, he was sent home to tell his mother he was safe. As he passed the remains of the '94 shop', he was asked by one of the rescue workers who lived at Smallford to go and tell his wife that he was safe but had no idea when he would be home.

The following day Jimmy was back at work and in most respects it was 'business as usual' but he was very conscious of the lucky escape he had had.

His second close encounter with the enemy took place on the evening of Friday, 22 September 1944. He had returned from work to the family home in Selwyn Crescent and had presumably been alerted by the siren as he had just helped his mother and sisters into the cupboard under the stairs for shelter. When the bomb fell at 8.48 p.m. Jimmy was struck by the blast and, when he regained his senses, found himself in the front garden with the door closed behind him. He and his family suffered a few odd cuts and bruises but they were so lucky compared with the occupants of the first pair of houses in Selwyn Crescent (Nos. 2 & 4). In one of those houses, Mr and Mrs Woodcock were killed although their daughter, Betty, was rescued and survived. Apparently she had been invited to a dance that evening but was not feeling well and decided to stay at home. That decision nearly cost her life.

Bomb damage in Selwyn Crescent, 22 September 1944

Because of reporting restrictions, the local newspaper could only identify the site as 'a housing estate in Southern England' and the time as 'on Friday evening.' It did, however, have some very human stories to tell. The most touching was that of LAC Ronald Knight who had left home, after a spell of leave, only about 20 minutes before the bomb fell demolishing his house and killing his wife and small daughter, Irene, along with the two neighbours. All attempts to contact LAC Knight on his way back to camp, to tell him of the tragedy, failed and he could not be informed until the next day in spite of 'efforts all through the night to trace him.' Towards the end of the report he was quoted as saying:

> I am quite sure everything that possibly could be done at the time was done. The ARP authorities and the Police carried out their work most satisfactorily and I cannot speak too highly of the way in which the local Council and its officials, particularly the Clerk, have handled things for me ...

A Mrs Snow achieved newspaper fame by telling the reporter how she had been boarding with the Knights but had left during the previous week—she was now pictured helping two of their nieces salvage possessions from the wreckage.

A nice moment was captured as Mrs Cox said 'God bless you' to two women friends who had left their own household work to come and help clear up.

'Who wouldn't help at a time like this?' replied her more fortunate friend. Meanwhile Mr Cox, with a cut on his head, was trying to sweep his garden path clear of broken glass. Incidentally, the report mentions two unnamed friends of the Cox family who were living there at the time because they had been bombed out of their home in London by a flying bomb. Such movement of population must sometimes have created problems in accounting for, and naming, disaster victims. In late February 1944, the wardens had tried to conduct a house-to-house Census to assist possible rescue work but it had been viewed with suspicion by householders who felt that it was a means of seeking more opportunities for billeting in their homes.

Another appealing human story was captured by the reporter when a happy, smiling bride 'despite the ordeal of the night before ... stepped out of a damaged house to drive away to her wedding in a car bedecked with the usual white ribbon.' It was later noted in the Council Minutes that a local baker had provided a substitute wedding cake within an hour of hearing about what had happened.

A mobile laundry unit (one of ten doing similar work throughout the country) owned and staffed by Lever Brothers as war service, arrived and at once started work on bundles of washing with the invitation to 'get your washing together and we'll do it for you.' One of the relief workers, Miss Bennett, highlighted a problem in using vehicles to support rescue work in hours of darkness as shattered glass punctured tyres and rendered the vehicles useless. She therefore advocated the sweeping of roads before allowing vehicles to proceed.

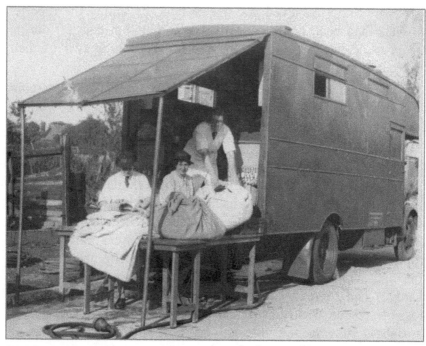

Mobile Laundry (Lever Bros.) at Selwyn Estate after Flying Bomb incident

The spirit of co-operation is epitomised by a couple of notices that were immediately erected on the estate. The first announced:

> The Northmet Company have offered to store free of charge residents' own electric cookers and/or electric washers. For particulars enquire within.

The second informed residents:

> Baths can be obtained at the 1st Aid Post, Memorial Hall, St Albans Road opposite the church throughout the day and by arrangement in the evenings. Towels and soap are available there.

The whole incident was characterised by bravery, community spirit and support from the surrounding area. Particular reference was later made to the courage of two local doctors, Jamieson and Burvill-Holmes, and District Surveyor, Mr J R Howarth, who went in through a tunnel to rescue victims who were buried in the rubble. Local feeling is summed up in a letter to the *Herts Advertiser* from the residents of the 'stricken estate':

> Sir – May we express our thanks through the medium of your paper to the voluntary wardens of Group 'C' of a neighbouring town, who came to our assistance so readily on Saturday and Sunday. We also thank the allied soldiers, NFS and WVS for their help to us at a time when we were too stunned to know where to turn.

A summary of the effects of this bombing stated that two houses had been destroyed, seven seriously damaged and 132 had minor damage (e.g. windows blown out). Four people had been killed, twelve seriously injured and around fifty slightly injured. A story circulating the town at the time, but which the present author has been unable to substantiate, suggested that the flying bomb was descending towards open land when it struck a flag pole at the Comet Hotel and was diverted towards the housing estate.

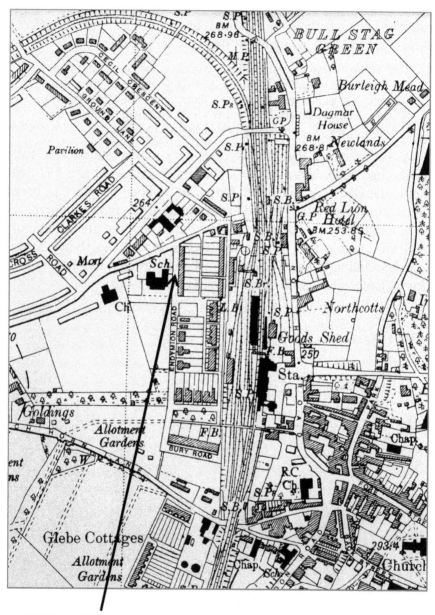

V1 bomb fell here, badly damaging St Audrey's School and houses in Endymion Road & Beaconsfield Road, and killing nine residents

Tuesday, 10 October 1944

T HE St Audrey's bomb, coming so soon (just over a fortnight) after that at Selwyn Crescent, was perhaps Hatfield's sternest test of endurance. Hardly had the funerals of the Selwyn victims taken place early in October, and the customary annual memorial service for those killed by enemy action at de Havilland's in 1940 been held in the parish church, when another flying bomb struck early on the morning of Tuesday, 10 October. The first entry in the ARP log-book at 04.40 a.m. read 'BANG' and heralded what was later to be designated 'a major incident'.

As the Rescue Party and ambulances swung into action at 5 a.m., they could hardly have envisaged the scope of injury and damage caused by the V1 which had hit a tree on the edge of the grounds of St Audrey's School and exploded, wrecking the school along with houses in Beaconsfield and Endymion Roads and trapping many residents in their own homes. With Mrs Williams organising the mobile canteen and Miss Lambert standing by at the Rest Centre, initial requests went out for assistance from Stanborough wardens, Brookmans Park ambulance and whatever help could be sent from Welwyn Garden City and de Havilland's.

Within the hour, there was support coming from various parts of the County, including two ambulances, eight fire appliances and fifty men promised from St Albans. At that time on an October morning, little could be done without lighting and the Incident Post organised by Mr Wright and Vic Cull kept requesting a mobile searchlight. Before daylight, extra ambulances arrived from de Havilland's, St Albans, Welwyn Garden City and Hatfield House. The mobile canteen was in operation and measures were in hand at the mortuary, and in preparation for cleaning and repair parties. Thought was also being given to furniture removal and storage. It seems slightly academic that Mr Oliver, the Headmaster, had to be contacted about the closure of the school!

St Audrey's School with bomb damage

John Groom, a long-standing Hatfield resident who was a teenager living in nearby Stonecross Road at the time, recalled seeing a flash and hearing the explosion. As his father was an ARP Warden, he quickly made his way with him over to the school, ignoring the considerable damage to their own home. Although it was not yet dawn, they had little difficulty in appreciating the extent of the damage. He was immediately approached by a member of the Heavy Rescue Team, Vin Berry, and they headed for the Council Depot at Mount Pleasant where John had recently started work. Notwithstanding the fact that John was still under age, they each jumped into a council lorry and drove them back to Endymion Road where they proceeded to salvage as much equipment as possible from the school.

Rescue vehicles and workers at Primrose Cottages, Endymion Road

Two-and-a-half hours after the bomb fell, a preliminary report established that there were already twenty-three hospital cases (mainly sent to Hill End Hospital) and one body in the mortuary, that of Mrs Curtis. Approximately 200 houses were damaged, together with the Council Offices, the Police Station and, of course, the senior school. There was extensive incidental damage in the area and all public services had been warned. The mortuary itself was slightly damaged and its door had to be forced by Alf Burgess on arrival. Some of the food shops on Brewery Hill (Great North Road) had suffered damage from the blast and emergency repairs to them were given priority that day. The Food Office itself was damaged but was still able to function.

Around 8 a.m. the names and addresses of the injured began to come in from the Rest Centre and First Aid Post, and further bodies were found. By 8.20 a.m. the summary of assistance available included three rescue parties, eight ambulances, one 'sitting-case' car, seven NFS pumps, sundry mutual aid and promises of help from the Regional Column and further Rescue

Parties as soon as they could get there. They arrived at 9.40 a.m. Help came in the form of lorries and men from the RAF at Mill Green, and later Panshanger and Woodside, while other offers came from repair and handymen at Oaklands, the Ministry of Works at Cambridge, Ekins and Co. (Builders) of Hertford and Messrs Blow and Peters of St Albans who were prepared to transfer twenty-five men working at Watford when they heard what had happened.

Primrose Cottages, Endymion Road

In the confusion, the local emergency arrangements, already tested so recently at Selwyn Crescent, held good. The help from de Havilland's and Olding's was immediate and practical, as was the support throughout the day from Hatfield House. Miss Bennett at Bush Hall offered emergency accommodation once official red tape had been cleared. The Hatfield Laundry not only offered its services for airing emergency supplies of blankets on their way to the Public Hall, it also collected laundry for washing free of charge on 10 and 11 October.

Minor panics took place in the search not only for missing people but also for everyday items such as soap, syrup, sugar, milk and slates for re-roofing, the last item eventually being provided by Lavers of St Albans. With co-operation, all-round problems were overcome as the day progressed and order was gradually established.

Once the casualties had been removed, the priorities were the feeding and shelter of the homeless and the protection of what was left of their homes where possible. A procession of lorries carried furniture not only to Tingey's and to Hatfield House but also to various Home Guard and Scout Huts around the area.

Mobile Canteen in Beaconsfield Road (Ted 'Pedlar' Palmer rightmost)

The Carmelite Convent in Batterdale provided firstly hot drinks, then breakfast and later dinners arranged specially for the homeless and those temporarily without cooking facilities, adjusting its school lunch programme to ensure that no-one went hungry. There was assistance from the County ARP canteen and an NFS canteen on the spot, while the British Restaurant provided meals for both bombed-out families and the influx of Civil

Defence workers from other areas. Camp-beds were organised from the ARP stores and, by nightfall, the Public Hall had been equipped with fifty beds, crockery, knives and emergency cooking facilities with staff standing by. If the siren were to go after 10 p.m., the WVS were on alert to report for duty.

One of the casualties, Harold Curtis, whose legs were crushed and who spent several months in hospital, retained vivid memories of the event ever after. He awoke, saw the flaming V1 overhead and jumped out of bed as the explosion took place. His parents were killed by the blast but thankfully his two sisters in another bedroom suffered only very minor injuries and shock.

He recounted a remarkable story of a bottle of whisky which survived among the debris. The bottle, already over fifty years old, had been given to his father by a local resident and was being kept to celebrate the end of the war. It was collected up with the other family possessions by the salvage workers and stored in Hatfield Park until they were rehoused. The unopened bottle remained in the possession of the family fifty years later.

The victims ranged in age from Mrs Skeggs, who was in her seventies, to little Colin Willson aged eighteen months. Young Colin died in hospital the following night while his older brother, David, suffered injuries which left him blinded. Mr and Mrs Curtis who are referred to above, were well-established local residents. He was described as 'an old soldier of the last war' and well-known to local residents as caretaker at the Public Hall. He had joined the Civil Defence Service at the outbreak of the war, later taking up full-time ARP duties and becoming store-keeper at the local ARP stores. Henry Saunderson was killed in his home, although his father and sister were rescued from the house and taken to hospital.

Unfortunately, Henry Saunderson Snr also died from his injuries later in hospital. George Dodsworth, a married man, believed to have been directed to the area from Spalding for war-work was another victim. He was lodging with Mr and Mrs Morgan both of whom were seriously injured. Donald William Pinder, a married man in his late thirties, died from his injuries incurred when he was hit by a flying door. It was reported that his wife and young son were safely in the shelter of their pantry. The ninth victim was Mr William Hills. As residents reluctantly left their shattered homes, one was seen to write on his severely damaged front door, 'We don't like to leave but look out Hitler on Victory Day.'

Funeral at St Luke's Church of one of the victims (possibly Mrs Curtis)

This devastating event, close to the heart of the community, was felt deeply by so many people but everyone had rallied round in a way which was a credit to the town. At the ensuing Special Council Meeting a week later, Councillor Doust-Smith, who was Chief Warden and Chairman of the National Emergency Committee, was unstinting in his praise not only of the Council Officers and the emergency services but also of the:

> townsfolk of Hatfield ... their courage and endurance, their quiet sense of doing their duty, and the wonderful desire of those who were stricken to help those who had been worse stricken. ... Hatfield

had suffered, and Hatfield came to the rescue ... not only Hatfield town but all parts of the district.

Appreciation was expressed for all the aid received from the surrounding area, particularly the neighbourliness of Potters Bar UDC which took over responsibility for certain incidents while Hatfield was preoccupied with its own disasters.

The loss of St Audrey's School was of particular significance as it must be remembered that this was the only secondary school in the town in those days. The setting up of alternative arrangements for the children of secondary-school age was therefore a high priority. Staff worked hard to recover materials and equipment and by the following Monday (16 October), lessons were able to recommence. Emergency classrooms had to be found and the Public Hall was again pressed into use for this purpose. Two classrooms were set up in the Court House and yet more accommodation was made available in some temporary huts. With classes so widely dispersed, administration must have been a nightmare for the Headmaster who was initially operating from a temporary office in the Old Town on the corner of Batterdale and the Great North Road.

All residents were loud in their praise of the speed and efficiency of the rescue services. The *Herts Advertiser* spoke of the 'moving scenes' at the Memorial Service at which many of those who took part in the rescue were represented. This service, on Saturday 14 October, in the Parish Church was marked by 'masses of flowers from various organisations and from friends and neighbours.' Prayers were said for not only the bereaved relatives but also for those nine men, sixteen women and five children who were seriously injured and for whom life would never again be the same.

The aftermath of these bombings could be found in the local papers as the fifth winter of the war approached. In December, a resolution of the Hatfield Rural Council called on the Rural Housing Conference to be held in Hertford to press for the immediate release of building-trade operatives in the Services to enable greater progress to be made with housing repairs. From the end of October 1944, the local Council had made it a matter of 'absolute priority' to rehouse the homeless and repair other homes damaged by the raids, but it was a slow business with both materials and labour in short supply.

In late January 1945, a call went out from the WVS for any kind of household goods 'from an ash-tray to a garden roller.' This was part of the 'Good Neighbour Scheme' run by the WVS to help bombed-out families return to normal. Three Hertfordshire depots were set up, one of which was at Hatfield, and people could qualify for help on a points system according to the extent of their bomb damage.

This assistance was later acknowledged in letters sent individually and collectively to thank the Council, the organisers and all participating in the scheme. Such a letter, dated March 1945, read:

> The bombed-out people would like to thank the local Council for all they have done for us. We don't know what we would have done without you and we also thank the WVS as we more fortunate ones settle down in our respective new homes. We realise the vast amount of work they have been doing on our behalf, and the many useful gifts they have collected for us are most welcome, as there are so many things we cannot buy. So, thanks also to the people who have kindly given those things from their homes. We do appreciate all that has been done for us.

The official view of the scheme, expressed by Miss Tubbs, the Hatfield Centre Organiser, was that it was working:

> terrifically well. ... We have now really fixed up most of those who have been rehoused locally. Once the local residents have been fixed up the gifts will go to help other areas which have suffered in the raids.

Another small example of 'good coming from evil' was the use made at de Havilland's of a crashed flying bomb displayed to help raise £1,000 towards the RAF Benevolent Fund and their own

Troops Gift Fund. From the fall of the first flying bomb in June through the second half of 1944, with the more serious incidents involving thirteen civilian fatalities and general disruption, this was perhaps the period of the war when the town and its people were most grimly united in the face of the enemy.

FROM the beginning of 1945, a change of atmosphere began to be felt in Hatfield, reflecting the national feeling that at last the war would soon be over and it would then be possible to get on with the business of living a normal life again. The snowy conditions early in the New Year with attendant power cuts could not dispel the growing optimism, and great fun was had by the young and the not-so-young on the toboggan runs on the Green Hill and Elephant Dell in Hatfield Park.

In April, the first reports came of Hatfield Prisoners of War arriving home. Released from Germany were Geoff Maddams (RAF) of Bury Road and Leslie Stebbings of Stonecross Road. By May, victory in Europe was assured and official and unofficial celebrations were widespread.

> Flags and bunting sprang up everywhere as if by magic, and Fore Street and Salisbury Square, where every house boasted one or more flags ... presented a particularly striking scene. Children, who were given two days holiday on 8 and 9 May, walked the streets waving flags and most people sported big red white and blue rosettes. A Union Jack bravely fluttered from the top of a chimney stack of a V-bombed cottage in Endymion Road. Many bonfires in the Stonehouse area were lighted on Monday night and were followed by a huge victory bonfire in Hatfield Park on VE Day. Children's sports, singing and dancing in the Old Palace, thanksgiving services in St Etheldreda's and the other churches, local factories closed ... all these things helped to underline the general relief and relaxation of tension. 'Hitler' gave the Nazi salute for the last time before he went up in smoke at the top of the 25ft high victory bonfire in Hatfield Park. An almost life-size effigy, made by Mr and Mrs Wallis and

> Mrs Watford, made a noisy departure ... as one thunder flash had
> been tucked into his hand and another into the seat of his pants!

Regrettably, even the VE Day celebrations were tinged with sadness as a result of an incident involving an evacuee from Alexandra House. On the day after the celebrations, he had dropped a lighted piece of paper into an empty petrol drum which exploded, injuring him very seriously. Records show that the boy was still in hospital in January 1946 and the case was being handled by family solicitors.

Towards the end of May, a meeting of the Rural District Council considered the detailed list of damage, deaths and injuries in their area:

- 503 Air Raid incidents in the District
- 34 Civilians killed
- 135 Civilians injured
- 1,608 Properties damaged of which
- 254 demolished or seriously damaged

In addition, a further 59 local Service Personnel—58 men and one woman—are commemorated at the Hatfield War Memorial opposite Hatfield Station. A further 22 men, who were patients at Hatfield House, are commemorated at the Hatfield Park War Cemetery, Great North Road, Hatfield. These figures include one man, J H F Scrope, whose name appears on both of the above memorials.

The meeting was anxious to extend praise and thanks to all for their contribution to the success of the war effort. It was decided that special letters of thanks should be sent to the Chief Warden and the Head Wardens and another should be sent to Mr Winston Churchill, congratulating him on the end of the war in Europe.

The Chairman also referred to the local personalities whose names had appeared in the Honours List, particularly the Council's own Clerk, Edgar Cull, who was awarded the MBE. He paid tribute to Mr Cull's devoted service to the town throughout the war. It was resolved to send congratulations to two other local men whose names appeared in the List, the local ARP Controller,

Mr Wright, on receiving the BEM and Mr Geoffrey de Havilland, the chief test pilot and eldest son of Sir Geoffrey de Havilland, whose award was not specified in the press report. Mr Wright was to receive a further surprise when his own wardens took advantage of a 'social' in the Old Palace to present him with an engraved silver cigarette case and lighter. The social, held to mark the Civil Defence change-over from war to peace, was attended by Lord and Lady Salisbury, the Deputy Chief Constable and his wife, Mr John Lockley, Chairman of the RDC, Mr and Mrs Chappell and Mr Cull.

Street Party at Wellfield Road, 1945

Change was in the air throughout the locality and the whole nation. At the end of May, the boys from Alexandra House who were about to return to their homes wrote to many of the townspeople thanking them for their friendliness during the three years of their evacuation. In June, a party was held to commemorate the closing down of the wartime Rest Centre at the Carmelite Convent.

Hatfield House was no exception to the general trend and was once again in the forefront of developments as the first Civil Resettlement Unit for ex-Prisoners of War and the HQ for Civil Resettlement Planning. The ex-PoWs could spend up to three months on a course in the workshops (located in the Old Riding Stables) where they could refresh their former trade skills or learn new ones. There was provision for lectures in the Old Palace and visits to local factories, etc. In July 1945, a visit to the new unit by their Majesties the King and Queen provided a surprise for local people as well as encouragement for the men undertaking training.

Football team at Hatfield House when it was a Civil Resettlement Unit, 20 March 1946

There were, of course, still problems, as envisaged by Mr Wright at his presentation, when he hoped that the spirit of comradeship which had been so great during the war years would not be lost with the advent of peace, but would continue to be used for the benefit of the town in the difficult period which lay ahead. Delays in the rebuilding of St Audrey's School and continuing housing problems, plus uncertainties created by the Abercrombie Report with its projected 'new town' in the district, all led to anxiety. The change of government ministers following the General Election was given as the reason for the delay in commencing the rebuilding of the town's only secondary school.

It may have been as a result of this local pressure that the site was soon cleared. An artist's impression of the new school was put on display at Tingey's Corner House in August 1945 and the new building opened in 1946.

However, the impending problems and uncertainties were not allowed to blight the British Legion Fête held in the grounds of Hatfield House early in July, or the giant picnic in the Park (reported to be the biggest ever held in the town) which was a victory-treat for the youngsters of Hatfield when the war against Japan ended in August. The Japanese accepted the terms of surrender on 14 August and, although the ceremony of signing the surrender document did not take place until 2 September, there was no reason for delaying the celebrations.

VJ Day itself was initially quiet—a day of thanksgiving when people flocked to church—but after that, a crescendo of celebrations began, culminating in the 'Picnic' on the following day. On VJ Night, the residents of Crawford Road were to be found dancing in the street to music from the wireless! The next afternoon, street parties were held throughout the town and in the Park.

> Over 2,400 children were given a big tea with sandwiches, cakes buns, fruit, sweets, nuts and dates, with mugs of lemonade to help it down. They ran races with special victory zest. Everywhere in the Park were children—small children, big children, thin children and chubby children, children with rosettes, children without them, but no children without a smile. And heaps of parents too.

An emergency meeting had produced fifty local ladies to do the catering and a committee of men to run the sports. Later, there was dancing around the 30 ft high bonfire (built by men of the RAF) to music broadcast from a van lent by de Havilland's.

The following Sunday there was a Victory Parade in the afternoon from the North Front of Hatfield House to the Parish Church, followed by a civic service of thanksgiving which was attended by members of the Council, the Civil Defence Services and representatives of all the local organisations that had done so much during the war.

The Civilian Defence personnel assembled outside the Court House, St Albans Road

RURAL DISTRICT COUNCIL OF HATFIELD.

DISBANDMENT OF CIVIL DEFENCE SERVICES.

Civil Defence Clothing & Equipment.

Whole and part-time members are allowed to retain the following items of Clothing and other equipment which have formed a personal issue.-

Steel Helmet.	Eyeshields.
Respirator.	Anti-Gas Ointment.
Uniform as issued.	

It will be a condition of retention of uniform that all badges and other insignia (except war service chevrons and wound stripes) are to be removed before it is worn on unofficial occasions.

Gum Boots, Oilskin Garments and any other equipment are not a personal issue and must be handed in to the responsible head of the Service and a receipt obtained.

EDGAR F. CULL.
Clerk.

Council Offices,
Hatfield.
1st May, 1945.

RURAL DISTRICT COUNCIL OF HATFIELD

COUNCIL OFFICES,
HATFIELD,
HERTS.

1st May, 1945.

To all Members of the
Civil Defence Services.

CIVIL DEFENCE GENERAL SERVICES.
DISBANDMENT OF WAR ORGANISATION.

The Council have been notified of the Government's decision that as from the 2nd May, 1945, the Civil Defence General Services are to be disbanded, and from that date part-time members are formally relieved of all obligations to perform Civil Defence duties.

We desire to express our very high appreciation of the services you have rendered to this District during a period of the greatest danger and strain that this Country has had to endure through the whole of its momentous and magnificent history. With God's help we have succeeded in enduring to the victorious end.

On behalf of the inhabitants of the Rural District of Hatfield we offer our thanks and gratitude to you for the services you have so cheerfully, steadfastly and voluntarily rendered. May we hope that the close relationship and understanding between the Council, its officers, the members of the Civil Defence Services and the public generally, which the tragic years of the War have fostered, will continue during the happier years of peace now about to dawn upon us, and that a more lively interest may be promoted thereby in the affairs of Local Government.

Wishing you all personal prosperity and happiness in the future.

Yours sincerely,

JOHN LOCKLEY,
Chairman of the Council.

E. C. DOUST-SMITH,
Chief Warden and Chairman of
National Emergency Committee.

102

Appendix A Hatfield Military Fatalities

<u>Commemorated at Hatfield War Memorial[17]</u>

Ager, Charles Peter—Driver REME, July 1944, England
Alderson, Richard C—Maj, Coldstream Gds, June 1944, Italy
Allen, Robert William—Petty Officer, RN, July 1943, Tobruk
Ballance, Denis Charles—L Aircraftsman, RAF, June 1941, England
Barber, Alfred Downes—Pte, Kings Regt, Jan 1945, Greece
Boxall, Frederick William—L Corporal, RE, Mar 1946, England
Brace, Richard Stanley—Private, RAOC, Pri Of War, 1942
Bracey, Walter—Lance Corporal, RE, April 1943, Nth Africa
Brownsell, John Stewart—Sergt, RAFVR, Jan 1942, England
Collie, Thomas P—Gunner, Royal Artillery, July 1943, Sicily
Cox, Frank Geoffrey—Flying Officer, RAF, Dec 1943, Berlin
Currell, Albert—Fusilier, R Scots Fus, Oct 1944, N W Europe
Drage, Quentin Lovell—Captain (MC), RHA, Sept 1944, Italy
Eagles, Arthur J—Royal Artillery, December 1942, Bombay
Elliott, Geoffrey Jack—CSM, R Signals, Jan 1947, India
Elliss, Alfred C—S Lt, RNVR, Fleet Air Arm, Aug 1944, England
Ewington, Stanley James—Private, RAOC, Nov 1944, Italy
Flitney, Doris M—WAAF, October 1946, England
Flitney, Ernest L—Pte, Beds & Herts Regt, June 1943, Burma
Foster, William Patrick—Flight Sergt, RAF, Oct 1944, Burma
Fuller, Herbert Almond—Pte, Beds & Herts Regt, P of War, Japan
Gant, Basil E—Pte, Worcester Regt, May 1940, France
Gaylor, Arthur A—L Cpl, Beds & Herts Regt, May 1940, Dunkirk
Gaylor, Henry G—Cpl, Beds & Herts Regt, Nov 1941, Tobruk
Greenham, Arthur H—Pte, Army Air Corps, June 1943, Sicily
Hall, Ronald Frank—Flight Sergt, RAF, May 1941, Crete
Hill, Kenneth A—L Sick Bay Attendant, RN, Jan 1943, N Atlantic
Hobbs, Ivor Kenneth—Pte, Somerset L Inf, Mar 1945, Germany
Jarmain, Raymond L—RFM, King's RRC, Apr 1943, Tunisia
Kendle, Frank Charles—L Cpl, Beds & Herts, May 1944, Burma
Laurence, Alan Robert—Sergt, Nav, RAFVR, Dec 1943, Europe
Lawrence, Ronald William—Sergeant, RAF, June 1940, France
Longhurst, William A—L Cpl, Corps M Police, Mar 1945, Germany
Minchin, Denis—Captain, Royal Artillery, 1940, England

---

[17] Abbreviations are as they appear on the actual memorial

103

May, Robert Seayears—Sqn Leader, RAF B Command, Apr 1943
Neale, Alfred Thomas—L Corporal, RE, Oct 1942, El Alamein
Nichols, Alfred Edward—Corporal, RAF, Nov 1945, England
Nicholas, Edward Charles—Pte, Somerset L Inf, Apr 1945, Holland
Parkinson, Jack Stanley—Sergt, Durham L Inf, Nov 1944, Italy
Payton, Sidney Thomas—Sapper, R Engineers, June 1940, France
Priestman, John Reeve T—Lt, Lincoln Regt, Mar 1943, Nth Africa
Quincey, James William—Sergt, Pilot, RAF, Mar 1941, Germany
Randall, Harry—L Cpl, R Corps of Signals, Apr 1943, Burma
Rourke, Cyril Herbert—Sergeant, RA, April 1941, Mid East
Scrope[18], John Henry Francis—Tech Asst Aerodynam, de Havilland, Aug 1943
Sear, Geoffrey A W—L Cpl, Duke of Wellington's RAC, July 1944, India
Sheppard, Benjamin Quinney—Sergeant, RAF, Dec 1940, England
Smith, Bernard Wilmot—Sergeant Pilot, RAF, Mar 1945, Ancona
Smith, Roland Jack—Sergeant Observer, RAF, July 1942, Germany
Storey, Frederick A—AB, HMS Sub Syrtis, Mar 1944, Drowned at Sea
Thompson, Richard Mc Kinley—Royal Marines, May 1945, Hamburg
Tyler, John—Sergeant, Monmouth Regiment, Dec 1944, Holland
Venables, Joseph Albert—Lance Sergeant, RE, Oct 1944, Holland
Wallis, Robert Wilfred—RFM, Rifle Brigade, July 1944, Italy
Watt, Sidney Miller—Bombardier, RA, P O War, July 1945, Sarawak
Weedon, Frederick N—Pte, Queen's Royal Regt, June 1944, Caen
West, Gerald Arthur—Flying Officer (DFM), RAF, Dec 1943, Berlin
Williams, Alfred A—Private, RAMC, Sept 1943, Malaya
Woodcock, David George Olney—Captain, KOYLI, Feb 1944, Anzio

---

[18] Buried at Hatfield Park War Cemetery (see below)

Hatfield War Memorial

Hatfield Park War Cemetery

Died at Military Hospital, Hatfield House – Commemorated at Hatfield Park War Cemetery, Great North Road, Hatfield[19]

Askey, H—Gunner, Royal Artillery, 8th December 1939, Age 39

Bird, W F—L Sjt, 33rd Searchlight Regt, RA, Lately 19th Co of Lond Regt, 22nd December 1940

Broom, W H—Squadron Leader, Navigator, Royal Air Force, 12th May 1944, Age 24

Brownsell, J S—Sergeant, Wireless Operator/Air Gunner, Royal Air Force, 16th January 1942, Age 21

Budler, J F C—Driver, Royal Army Service Corps, 13th December 1943, Age 43

Bullick, R—Private, The Suffolk Regiment, 26th February 1942, Age 51

Chandler, A—Private, The Suffolk Regiment, 9th September 1941

Dixon, S G—Private, Buckinghamshire Battn, Oxf & Bucks LI, 16th January 1941

Eagles, A H—Corporal, Royal Signals, 21st September 1941

Edwards, C—Serjeant, The Royal Fusiliers, 28th May 1946

Hoad, J— Private, of Canada Pioneer Corps, 24th January 1944

Jones, A J—WO I (RSM), Corps of Military Police, 6th August 1943, Age 38

Jones, D W—Private, The Hampshire Regiment, 11th December 1940

Knudson, K A—Ldg Aircraftman, U/T Pilot, Royal Air Force, 8th October 1941, Age 25

Moore, W—Ldg Aircraftman, Royal Air Force, 2nd September 1941, Age 18

Scrope, J H F[20]—23rd August 1943, Age 24

Seyderhelm, E E—L Sjt, Royal Army Ordnance Corps, 18th June 1946, Age 31

Smart, A—Gunner, 94th (Dorset & Hants) Field Regt, RA, 8th August 1940, Age 21

Walsh, J—L Cpl, Corps of Military Police, 7th November 1940, Age 25

Williams, T—Private, Royal Army Medical Corps, 27th February 1943

Wilmot, W J J[21]—Petty Officer, RN, HMS Aurora, 6th August 1947, Age 27

Wilson, J—S Sjt, Royal Artillery, 2nd February 1942, Age 38

---

[19] Abbreviations are as they appear on the actual headstones

[20] Also commemorated on Hatfield War Memorial (see above)

[21] Headstone, but buried in St John Churchyard, Digswell

Appendix B Hatfield Civilian Fatalities

3 October 1940 – de Havilland Bomb

Allen, Horace Frederick George
Bowles, Jack Eric
Collom, Richard Hockley
Easter, William James Cuffley
Gibbins, Alfred Leonard
Harrod, William Edward
Henry, Eric Reginald
Parry, Reginald
Scott, Anthony James
Smith, John Holmes
Waddingham, Alfred Edward

Arlidge, Frank Joseph
Bush, Henry Herbert Stacey
Dawson, Owen Kendall
Fordham, Cecil Harry
Gibbs, Frederick William
Hartley, Frederick
Norfolk, Charles
Pretty, Ernest Frederick
Sim, William James Geddes
Toop, Lionel Alfred

22 September 1944 – Selwyn Crescent Bomb

Knight, Irene
Woodcock, Ernest

Knight, Ruth
Woodcock, Minnie

10 October 1944 – St Audrey's Bomb

Curtis, Dorothy May
Dodsworth, George
Pinder, Donald William
Saunderson, Henry
Willson, Master Colin

Curtis, Stephen
Hills, William
Saunderson, Henry James
Skeggs, Jane

Bibliography

Printed Works

Birmingham Post, December 1939.

Gray, H John, *Cricketers and Cricket in Hatfield in the 20th Century (1897–1945)*, unpublished typescript.

Herts Advertiser & St Albans Times, various editions, 1939–45.

Hook, Elizabeth, *Growing Up in Hatfield before 1945 (Book 4)*, privately published by Frank Cox for Hatfield Local History Society, 2000.

Kingsford, Peter, *The Labour Movement in Hatfield 1918–1970*, Peter W Kingsford, 1988.

McKee, Alexander, *The Mosquito Log: The Inside Story of the Much Loved 'Mossie'*, Souvenir Press, 1988.

Pankhurst, Terry, *When The Bombs Dropped: The story of the de Havilland Factory Bombing, 3rd October 1940*, privately published by Terry Pankhurst for Hatfield Local History Society, 2010.

Ramsay, Winston G, *The Blitz Then & Now (Vol. 2)*, Battle of Britain Prints International Ltd, 1988.

Sainsbury, J D, *Hertfordshire's Soldiers: A survey of the Auxiliary Military Forces raised in Hertfordshire from 1757 to the Present Day*, Hertfordshire Local History Council, Hitchin (Herts.), 1969.

Other References

War Memorial, Great North Road, Hatfield.

Hatfield Park War Cemetery, Great North Road, Hatfield.

Ordnance Survey maps, 1937 & 1948–49.

INDEX

Note: Page numbers in *italics* indicate illustrations.
Appendix A and the Bibliography are not included in the index.

Park 27, 47, 48, 99
Riding School 33, 49
victory celebrations 95, 99
see also Military Hospital; War
   Cemetery
Hawkshead House 57
Henry, Eric Reginald 107
Hertford 60, 88, 92
   Junkers crash 59, *59*
Herts Advertiser 5, 7, 9-10, 13, 18,
   42, 83, 92
Herts Public Assistance
   Committee 16
Hewson, Capt. C. J. 74
Hill, Billie 49
Hill End Hospital 53, 60, 87
Hills, William 91, 107
Hitler, Adolf
   cartoon *iv*
Hobbs, A. E. 23
Holidays at Home 49-50
Home Guard 27, *28*, *54*, *72*, 73-4,
   75-6
   Band 48
   13th Battalion 27, 74
   14th Battalion 27, *28*, 74
Honister House 38
Hook, Elizabeth 29
Hopkyns, Mrs 16-17
hospitals 47
   Bush Hall 29, 31
   Hill End 53, 60, 87
   isolation 13
   London 17, 36
   Stalingrad Hospital Fund 38,
      69, 70
   US Forces General Hospital 40
   see also Military Hospital

housing 4, 18, 51, 92-3
Howarth, J. R. 82
Howe (fireman) 71
Hurricane aircraft 54

I

ICI 35
identity cards 20
identity numbers 2

J

Jack Olding and Co. Ltd 51, 88
   factory 1, 4, *54*, 54-5, 74
Jamieson, Dr 82
Jeffries (fireman) 71
Jenkins, Hugh *14*
Johnson (carpenter) 29
Junkers aircraft 57-60, *59*, 61

K

Kindersley, Lord 47
Knight, Irene 80, 107
Knight, Ronald 80
Knight, Ruth 80, 107
Knowles, C. 18
Knowles, C. S. 9

L

Labour Party 37, 70
Lambert, Miss 85
Laundry, Hatfield 88
Lavers of St Albans 89
Lawrence, Brian
   childhood 1-3, *1*
Lemsford 9
Lemsford Road Halt 52, 53, 68
Leonard, Mrs M. P. G. 9

113

S

Salisbury, James Cecil, 4th
 Marquess of *vi*, 17, 21,
 27, *30*, 31, 33, *44*, 46,
 47, 48, 70, 97
Salisbury, Lady Cicely Alice
 Gore, 4th Marchioness
 of *vi*, 13, 21, 27, 29, *30*,
 97
 patient's letter to 34
Salisbury Hall 61
Salisbury Square 95
Salute the Soldier Week 49
salvage 39-44, 68
Salvation Army Mission Hall 52
Saunderson, Henry 90, 107
Saunderson, Henry James 90, 107
Savings Committee, Hatfield 47
schools
 Dellfield 74
 evacuees 5, 7, 9, 10-11
 Green Lanes 65
 Newtown 65
 Stroud Green, Hornsey 9, 12
 see also St Audrey's School
Scott, Anthony James 107
Scout Troop 74
 Cub Scouts 41
scrap-iron 41-2, 44
Scrope, John H. F. 35, 62, 96, 106
Secker (Salisbury's agent) 31
Secker, H. J. 9
Selwyn Crescent
 bombed 78, 79-83, *80*, *82*, 85
 fatalities *listed* 107
Selwyn housing estate 4, 51
Shade, David 65
shelters 1, 18-20, 63-4

Anderson 20, 64
ARP 17-18, 50
Haldane 64
Morrison 2, 64
tunnels 64
Sherriff, L. C. 18
Sherriff's Mill 76, 77
shops 21, 66-8
 Mutual Assistance
 Committee/Pacts 66-7
Sim, William James Geddes 107
Skeggs, Jane 90, 107
Smallford 3
Smith, Brian 43-4
Smith, John Holmes 107
Snow, Mrs 81
soldiers 1, 55, *59*, 67
 Salute the Soldier Week 49
 Wounded Soldiers Scheme 37
 see also Military Hospital; War
 Cemetery
Southampton Fire Brigade 71
Spitfire Fund, Hatfield 45
Spitfires 45, 54
St Albans 48, 52, 85
St Albans Co-operative Society 24
St Audrey's School 38, 45, 47, 48,
 79
 bombed *84*, 85-92, *86*
 fatalities *listed* 107
 Memorial Service 92
 aftermath 92-3
 rebuilt 98-9
St Etheldreda's (Parish Church)
 46, 85, 92, 95, 99
St John's Ambulance Brigade 21,
 46
 Red Cross and St John's 37, 39

Lightning Source UK Ltd.
Milton Keynes UK
UKHW01f1037210618
324586UK00006B/678/P